Presented as Faultless

Presented as Faultless

Da'Shay Perry

Cover photos by Motelewa Smith.
Cover design by LACreative
Page design by Win-Win Words

**Some of the names in this book have been changed to protect
the true identities of those involved.**

ISBN: 978-0-692-94341-0

Printed in the United States of America

To all my babies! De'Asia, DeBria, Brianna, Brooklyn, and Shayla. I love you all with every inch of my soul. May God cover, guide, and protect each of you as HE has done for me!!

Contents

Acknowledgments

I WOULD FIRST LIKE TO THANK GOD FOR BEING MY STRENGTH. Without him I couldn't possibly have been able to complete this trying assignment.

Second, I would like to thank my mother, DeAnna Bean, even though I felt she was very hard on me growing up. She helped me evolve into the woman that I am today. I constantly pray for the two of us, and I'm happy and thankful for how I've seen prayers manifested in your life. I love you and am forever grateful; I wouldn't ask for anyone else to be in the space or position as my mother.

My father, Jeffrey Perry; where would I be without you? I ask you this frequently. I am thankful for your voice in my life and our relationship that has grown so much; you've talked me out of a lot of turmoil. I could never repay you.

To my grandparents who are as fine as wine, Leroy and Olivia Bean. Grandma, thank you for always being by my side, whether I was near or far. You've always understood my pain and have such great comfort to give. Good, bad, or indifferent, you've been there for me. I love you forever and a day!!! Grandpa, thank you for being a father. Your few words have always spoken big volumes!! I appreciate your sternness. I love you both so much!

My baby sisters—De'Asia, Brianna, and Bria—you mean so much to me. De'Asia, you've impacted my life more than you know. You actually saved it! I'll never forget that. Thank you for loving me even when I didn't love myself. Bria, you'll always be my big baby! Thank you for your tenderness, loving heart, and your compassion. You rock! Brianna, I am so glad about how our relationship has grown over the years. You are so amazing. I'm so proud of you beyond what you know. Thank you for being a listening ear in times of need. I love you all so much.

Uncles and aunts: Jimmy Bean, Jermaine Bean, Leanna Williams, Dianna Romine, Lisa Walder, Jamar Bean, Leroy Bean, Deborah Marbury, Leon Bean, Yogi Simmons, Diane Shackelford, Dana Shackelford, Dionne Shackelford, and Anita Branigan—thank you for all you did for my sisters and me as kids. Coming over to watch us, taking us or getting us from school, allowing us to come to your house . . . you name it! You all helped my mother in a *major way*!!! Thank you, from the bottom of my heart, thank you!

Aunt Doreen, my super woman! I love you so much!! You got my mind off so much as a child. Thank you for providing love and a cool environment for all the cousins growing up.

Sahresa Perry, thank you for *always* opening your home to me, more than once. You have such an amazing heart, God bless you.

To the *best* pastor on the planet—Bishop Joseph Walker!!! Where would I be if it wasn't for the spirit of God that is within you? There aren't enough words to describe the depth of my appreciation for you. Your ministry has truly changed my life! Since moving to Nashville and coming up under your leadership, I have been challenged to grow mentally, come into a full and deeper relationship with God, and pushed into my destiny. Thank you so much, Bishop, I greatly appreciate you.

To my godparent that God blessed me with entering into Nashville—Ms. Janice. I wish you were here to see what I've accomplished! *I did it*! I wrote the book. I am thankful for the time I got to spend with you. You'd be so proud of me. I miss our talks! I'll continue to make you happy.

Mama Lorie!!! Thank you for being that awesome figure in my life. I appreciate all your love and support over the years. You're so real, and I thank you for being open and transparent with me. I respect your realness. I love you!

Mama Cookie!! You are my love; thank you for your awesome spirit. I love you so much, and thank you for loving me, and for all your encouragement and motivating talks, which have really helped me. I'm so thankful for you and Papa Doug.

Doug and Michelle Nolan!! Where do I start? You two have blessed me in a tremendous way! In ways I can't even explain, I appreciate and love you two beyond what I can even comprehend. I am grateful for such an organic relationship.

To my friends who have witnessed all or some of this beautiful mess I wrote about. Candice Crenshaw, Rodney Baldwin, Jordan Brooks, Natalie Incorvia, Shantelle Sealey, Valerie Flores, Ciara Walker, and Briona Jackson. There's so much I want to individually say concerning each of you. I could write a book on how each of you has impacted my life in such an amazing way. You all were with me during my deepest darkest moments. You never judged, never gave up hope; instead, you encouraged me and so on. Thank you all for loving me in the midst of all this, seeing the best in me when I didn't see it; understanding transitional seasons; and *never* allowing me to settle no matter what. I love you, and greatness is waiting for us all!!!!!

Mike Towle, my editor. Thank you so much for your honesty throughout this whole process, thank you for all your help, your understanding, listening to my story, and working with me. Thank you so much.

Tressa Azarel Smallwood, my book consultant, *you are amazing*! Had I not met you, I'd still be journaling, saying "I've been working on this project for four years!" Thank you for the extra push and believing in me and helping this thing come to life! *God bless you*!

Brittany Pope, thank you for slaying my makeup for this cover, having me look "Faultless" and flawless. And to Mo, my photographer, for bringing the vision to life. Working with you was an awesome experience. Thank you both so, so very much.

Last but certainly not least, my "King Handsome," Jaron Spicer. Thank you isn't enough for you, but for lack of better words, I truly thank you! You've helped me throughout this whole process. You've traveled back down memory lane, confronted every situation, and tackled every hardship with me. You've dealt with so many tears and much more. The process definitely wasn't easy, and even when my past tried to come between us, you stood still, continued to love and fight with me. For that, I could never repay you. Thank you for loving and believing in me the way you do. I love you so much, and I look forward to the rest of our journey together. May God continue to bless us all forever and ever!

Though I may not have written about you all in the book, I want you to know that each of you has a very special place and have impacted my life in a major way. You've all contributed to who I am today. Again, I say, thank you. I'll love you all forever!

Introduction

"All things work together for good! Even unkind words
spoken against you are like distasteful seasoning
that helps your flavoring."
— HART RAMSEY

I T WAS AROUND 3:30 P.M. WHEN I RECEIVED THE PRECEDING Ramsey quote via text message on my phone. I was driving on the interstate, headed back to Nashville from Dayton, Ohio, after one of the *worst* experiences of my life! I was feeling empty, broken, unworthy, depleted, and downright lousy! My own foolishness, misjudgment, and idiocy had landed me in a complete mess.

Unfortunately, I had had a few of those moments. "Stupid bitch, dumb bitch" kept replaying in my head. Those were the words that had been fired at me thirteen hours earlier, before I left for home.

Driving in a daze, I was trying to make sense of it all. "How could he do that to me?" I asked myself. "No one has ever treated me that way! How could he almost take my life?"

I had just become a victim of domestic violence; not for

the first time, but for the second. This time was different. In the blink of an eye, one bad decision had almost cost me my life! My spirit and flesh were warring at one another the whole four-and-a-half-hour drive home to Nashville. However, during it all, I felt a sense of comfort in a very distinctive way. A ray of sunshine peeked through a slightly cloudy sky, and it hit me right on the cheek. It was in that moment I felt that God had spoken to me. I knew I had to own up to the part I had played in this situation.

Tyrell wasn't my husband; I knew that! I knew from the moment we met exactly what he wanted and for what purpose he was in my life. He was there to teach me a lesson. I didn't want to accept that at that point and time in my life, though.

I, like many others, need and/or liked instant gratification. I also loved to give people the benefit of the doubt. In going a little deeper and being real about the situation, I was someone who clearly just wanted to do whatever it is they want to do— someone driven by lustful desires, someone who doesn't believe the stove is hot until they touch it. Yes, that was me!

A very small part of me believed Tyrell would change his thuggish ways. But as time went on (and it didn't take long), I came to the realization I shouldn't have been in that situation. I continued to deal with him; because of that, I got way more than I bargained for. That turned out to be a blessing in disguise, because of that, as well as numerous other events, I have landed exactly where I am today!

Consider some horrifying statistics regarding women and children today:

- More than 90 percent of sexual offenders are known and trusted by the child—a parent or relative, teacher, camp counselor, babysitter, or family friend. (www.childsafeeducation.com)

- Only one in ten children who are abused will ever tell anyone.

- A woman is battered every fifteen seconds, according to the FBI.

- Nearly 80 percent of girls who have been physically abused in their intimate relationships continue to date their abuser. Source: *Letters to Young Black Women*, a book by Daniel Whyte III and Meriqua Whyte.

- One in four children under the age of eighteen—a total of about 17.4 million—are being raised without a father, according to the U.S Census Bureau.

Although all these statistics are difficult to fathom, aside from the child-related stats, the most troubling thing when it comes to the abuse of women in relationships is that more young women today are allowing themselves to be mistreated, hurt, and neglected by unscrupulous men who either don't care for them or fail to treat them with love and respect. Many women engage in or allow something to happen to them that seems small at the time, but it ends up impacting the rest of their lives with devastating consequences; that *was* me.

This book is about a journey—my real, raw, and uncut journey to self-love and self-confidence. It is my story of grace, victory, and triumph. This book will shed light on the power of divine intervention! I wrote this book to help, impact, and motivate women and children to know that although I've made many mistakes along the way, I am a faultless beauty! (Jude 1:24). I believe in ACT, an acronym for one way to live life. I've learned that if you Acknowledge your mistakes, Confront the people or things that try to get you to go backward (as well as the voices that try to remind you of who you used to be or things that happened to you), and you Trust the plan—God's plan, your healing process will be easier and faster!! I am a living witness.

I invite you to explore some moments of my life with me. These are moments that God used to mold me. These are moments that led me to be pure, strong, gracious, *whole*, faithful, and steadfast. These are moments that encouraged me to be thankful for the wisdom and understanding that I received from every experience. I didn't know it at the time, but they in fact were moments that were preparing me for my destiny. Moments that equipped me for the people to whom I am assigned! I hope that you will read it, learn from it, and never live a defeated life again.

Part I: Pain

1
Covered in Grace

"Before I formed you in the womb, I knew you;
before you were born, I set you apart; I appointed
you as a prophet to the nations."
— JEREMIAH 1:5

M AW-MAW, WHAT ARE YOU DOING DOWN THERE?" I ASKED
that question of my grandmother as I stood up, wiping
the sleep from my eyes while trying to get them to focus. It
was still fairly dark out; there was just enough light to where I
could see Maw-Maw, and she could see me.

"I've been up praying" were the words that came from her
mouth.

This was a daily ritual for Maw-Maw.

"Come here, Shay-Shay!" she instructed.

There I was a curious, four-year-old girl who was inquis-
itive even at a young age. Maw-Maw's right hand on my right
thigh and left hand on my back helped pull me down and off
the bed, turning me around at the same time to position me
on my knees toward the bed. Maw-Maw took both of my
hands and placed them together in front of me.

Before she led me to close my eyes, she looked into them, saying, "This is what you do each day and night! Once in the morning, thanking God for allowing you to see another day, and again at night for getting you through your day."

"Yes, Ma'am," I replied.

I then fell into her arms for the warmest hug and sweetest kiss on the forehead, both of which I knew to expect from her. Gosh, everything was so simple back then. Maw-Maw was my angel. I spent time with her often. Just about every weekend, to be exact. Maw-Maw, who was my father's mom, was a pastor of a tiny church by the name of the New Holy Church in Christ in Dayton, Ohio.

I can remember going to the church like it was yesterday. It was a tiny, white church at the end of a dead-end street. Walking through the large, white double doors in the front, you'd see burgundy-ish carpet. Inside were vinyl-looking walls and hardwood pews painted white. The church didn't have any windows, and it probably seated only a hundred fifty to two hundred people. I always thought everyone in the church was really old. I always felt like I was the youngest one—perhaps I was!

Maw-Maw was extremely faithful to her church, the community, and her family. She was an amazing woman. I also remember watching Maw-Maw on the television as she would go to and speak at events or on a local TV talk show in Dayton. Almost every Sunday that I'd go with Maw-Maw to church, she would preach a sermon and people would come forward out of their seats to get their heads anointed with oil. This would be my double-dose day. That's what I would call it because we had our prayer sessions at home (nothing too extreme), at which time she would pray with and over me while anointing my head with oil. If it was a day where she was doing it at church, I knew to get up and follow the line that led to the middle in front of the altar, where Maw-Maw would stand singing an old-time hymn with the choir.

God is very intentional when he does what he does. I truly believe that all the time that Maw-Maw and I spent together was for a purpose greater than what I could comprehend or even think about at the time. The path ahead would be extremely rocky! Maw was simply fulfilling her task in covering me and praying that God would continue to have me in his hands, and instilling in me the importance of prayer!

I learned as I got older, just recently in my twenties to be exact, that God uses people as instruments to physically do his work. That's so when you're able to grasp what's actually going on, you'll be able to decipher the authentic meaning of divine intervention. Maw-Maw was truly one of God's instruments, but back then I saw her as my hero.

As I got a little older, when I was entering elementary school and then on to the early parts of middle school; there were times I would get into trouble. I did this a lot back then, mostly for lying as well as for poor grades in school. My mother didn't really know how to respond to it at first; at least that's what I assume. So, she would take me to my grandmother's for what I call an intervention. Prior to getting to Maw-Maw's on the car ride over, my mother would be livid, telling me how I would still be in trouble once I left my grandmother's house to return home.

Once I had arrived at Maw-Maw's, I always felt her place was like a breath of fresh air. Walking in the air was always so crisp and cool, as if God himself had breathed on you as soon as you entered. It was an inexplicable peace she engendered in her house. My mother and I would walk in one way and leave out another. Hmm, funny thinking about it now; that's truly how I knew I'd been in the presence of God.

Maw-Maw had a big, long, beige couch perched directly across from the front door—you couldn't miss it when walking into the house. There also were two pink chairs situated in front of the window, and that's where all our meetings took place. Back then I wasn't thinking on a spiritual level or all deep and drawn out; I just knew that when my mother and I went to Maw-Maw's, there were no whooping's for me.

Maw-Maw would talk with me, and she was calm about everything. She would look at me and tell me, "This isn't you." Leaving Maw-Maw's, I felt as if everything was great: I wasn't in trouble with my mother anymore, and I felt renewed. Sadly, after some time, I believe my mother had just given up on having talks with Maw-Maw. Perhaps she felt as if her talks weren't working anymore.

As time went on, my behavior got worse. I had gone through certain phases where I was stealing, fighting, getting suspended from school, and lying my tail off! I was a habitual liar. I was convinced at a young age there was something wrong with me simply because I would lie before I had even processed the question that was asked. The lie would come out of my mouth so fast it was like it wasn't even me that was in control.

That is one of the issues that my mother had with me. My lying was just for no apparent reason. Once I responded with the lie, something in me would feel so horrible for lying and want to answer with the truth, but I would be so embarrassed that I just would suppress those feelings. The same goes for fighting. I would get into fights and feel so horrible afterward. I would black out when getting into fights at school or in the neighborhood; then, once the fight was over, I would return to reality and feel *horrible*.

Looking back, I know I had to go through all of that. I now realize that some of the behavior might have led to the absence of my parents—my mother in the emotional sense and my father in all respects. By no means am I making excuses for some of the things that happened in my life and my reaction to them, especially when I got out of the adolescent years. I'm simply saying kids have a reason for acting out. Typically, there's a root rationale to the issue, and you will find out in the next chapter what my idea of that source, for me, could have been.

A Letter to Shay Shay

Dear Shay Shay,

Hey Beautiful, it's your older self. I am reaching out to you this far in advance because I think I should tell you some important things that will be useful for this lifelong journey on which you are about to embark. You're so full of joy and always so happy. You have a heart of gold, and you truly love everyone! I ask that you always—and I mean always—remain that way, no matter what! Always know that God has a purpose and a plan for you. Always look back and remember Maw-Maw, even in times when you don't talk to her as much as you once did. Remember those prayers; remember that she covered you; remember that there are angels fighting on your behalf and that you're never alone. Remember that your mother, father, and all your other family members truly love you. Always respect your mother. No matter what you two go through, know that you're her daughter, and she truly does love, care for and wants nothing but the best for you.

Honor your mother and father all the days of your

life no matter what!! Remember, you can't pick the hand you're dealt and you must love your parents just as they are! Don't be naïve; if something doesn't feel right, say it! If you have a funny feeling about something or someone—no matter what they say—be bold and confront it. Don't be afraid. Tell someone. Don't let people push you around in making you do things you don't want to do. You're not a puppet; you're a princess. You're not to be toyed with. You're smart. You're not a sex slave! You're worth more than that. You're royalty.

Know who you are! As you get a little older, don't be so hard on yourself! You're amazing; you're intelligent; you're loved; and you will live! You have a great future ahead of you, but the road just ahead of you is rocky. You will encounter strange things head-on at an early age. The key is to just hold on . . . hold on to everything Maw-Maw has instilled in you. What you don't know, and unfortunately won't realize until you get older, is that you have so much strength and so much resilience, and that God is truly on your side. He loves you.

Lastly, you have to be strong; you can't quit or give in—you have little sisters that are looking up to you. I can't reveal too much to you right now. I'll just tell you, you need to get your tough girl face on and prepare yourself for the fight of your life.

Until next time,
Da'Shay

2
Girl Interrupted

"For I consider that our present sufferings are not worth comparing with the glory that will be revealed in us."
— ROMANS 8:18

THE SUN ISN'T OUT YET, AND I'M JUST WAKING UP. I LOVE WAKING up each day. Something about seeing the sun come up has always excited me since I was a child. However, this time when I awoke, it was unlike any other; to be frank, this was a weird morning.

I woke up to an unexpected feeling on my face. Back and forth motions, slowly, back and forth. I noticed I could barely breathe, and the stench in my nose was a musky smell. I slowly opened my eyes and saw there was a woman on top of me. I closed my eyes and mouth extremely tight, and I remember thinking, "*Oh, my God*! She's trying to suffocate me."

I couldn't breathe. More importantly, I couldn't grasp the reality that a grown woman was sitting on my face. I couldn't understand why she was on top of me. I was a five-year-old, having just experienced a form of molestation for the first

25

time. As best as I can remember, that was the first and only time that that happened to me. An experience that isn't easily forgotten. I didn't really think much about that moment after it had happened until I got older and had been born again, but thoughts of threesomes did cross my mind at times, and I remember being intrigued by the thought.

Hmmm, why would I want to give up my body to someone else so freely? Or invite those unwanted spirits into my space? Why did I have the desire to do such things? Could it have been a seed that was planted in me long ago that produced these lustful desires? Although I didn't comprehend it at the time—keep in mind how young I was then—perhaps it was subconsciously in my mind? Maybe it was something that had been passed down in the form of a generational curse? Whatever it was, these thoughts and questions bounced around in my head a very long time, and for years I didn't see anything wrong with that. Without a doubt, I was ignorant to the consequences and repercussions of my holding onto those thoughts!

Although I didn't engage in those types of acts, those thoughts, along with others, circled in my mind like a revolving door at the time of my extreme brokenness. They stuck with me because I didn't cast them down through prayer, nor did I combat them with my knowledge of who I was and what I believed.

A few years later, around 2001, when I must have been eight or nine, my mother had enrolled me in a public school. It was Louise Troy Elementary School, which was connected to a middle school known as Miami Chapel. My mother and her seven siblings went to Miami Chapel, where all the teachers knew you as well as your entire family. So, if you got into trouble in class, it was very easy to relay the message to a parent, grandparent, or older sibling because there were so many points of contacts there.

At that young age, I was very chatty. I was often told to stop talking so much. I loved to talk. I remember so vividly having a conversation in the bathroom with a few of my friends that I even remember what I was wearing that day. I had on a long jean dress.

My friends and I always went to the bathroom around the same time each day. That was our favorite meeting spot. I am not sure what sparked this particular conversation on this day; we were talking about what we wanted to be in life once we grew up. The words that came out of my mouth were "I want to be the person who talks to people and helps them get through whatever it is they're going through. By telling them my story, I want to help them with all of their problems."

By the time I was in the fourth grade, I knew what I wanted to be. Maybe I didn't know the exact title of the profession or how God would have me working in that field, but I knew I wanted to talk with and help people. Maybe it meant being a psychologist, a counselor, a profession in the medical field, or perhaps even a hairdresser. Those are all the things I thought about becoming. I had no idea, though, what I was about to encounter over the next twelve to thirteen years—experiences, I suppose, that would prepare me for what I would be doing in life.

Today, I know that what I went through in those years was preparing me for what my soul wanted, for what I desired to be, and for what God had me on this earth to do: to help heal, deliver, and set free others because of my story. I had no idea that I would be chosen for something like this. I had several issues going against me in that regard; for one thing, like I mentioned in chapter 1, I was a fighter. I used to get into a lot of fights, and that got me into a lot of trouble. This might have been me just trying to be someone that I wasn't. Either that, or I was seeking attention.

My mother was a hustler, always working, *Constantly.* She had to provide for three girls. She worked and she worked hard. She made sure my sisters and I were taken care of and that we never missed a beat. Anything that my sisters and I wanted, we got. My mother did everything that she could do financially for my sisters and me. She was the sole breadwinner, and she was doing a damn good job! But, to me, there was one thing missing. At least that's how I felt back then: she was never there emotionally.

Once my clothes were packed, I would wait for my father to arrive. Hours would go by, and I would be still waiting. I'd go back into the room and ask my mom, "Has he called yet?"

I know my mother loved us, and she tried very hard to provide for three kids all by herself, but as a young woman I needed that emotional support. My father was in and out of my life. During my childhood years, he was around a decent amount, but as I grew older he drifted away. He was never consistently there in my life during my preteen through teen years! There were a few occasions when I did hear from him as I grew up. He would call me and tell me how he was on his way to come and get me. I would gather all my things. Once my clothes were packed, I would wait for my father to arrive. Hours would go by, and I would be still waiting. I'd go back into the room and ask my mom, "Has he called yet?"

"Nope," she'd reply.

I would wait longer! I just knew he was coming. My dad was my world. I would begin to call him, but I would only get his voicemail, which was already full. I would make call after call after call, and still no answer. I knew that he sometimes would even ignore the call. By the time night time came around, I was convinced he wasn't coming. That act of selfishness on his part was always disheartening to me as a child. Although my father was in and out of my life, I loved him then and still love him deeply. He could do no wrong in my eyes—which is still true to this present day—no matter how many times he lied, didn't show up, or let me down.

I was Daddy's little girl. When my father was in my life *as a child*, it usually consisted of his coming over to pick me up and take me shopping. He would spend hundreds of dollars on clothes and shoes, then we would go to dinner, shortly after which he dropped me off with my mother, or with one of my grandmothers; it just depended on who had me at the time.

At times like that, I would get dropped off back home with so many new things. It was as if I had just gone on a shopping spree. I would feel bad for my two other sisters that lived with me, De'Asia and De'Bria, because here I was coming home with all these new Jordans, Adidas, and Nikes. There also were new belts, lots of different types of coats (depending on the season), outfits, you name it! My baby sisters had nothing new, at least not as much as I got.

At times like this, I would tell my mother, "Don't worry about me." Depending on the season, if it was close to my birthday or Christmas I would tell her, "Don't worry about getting me anything." I felt I had enough.

Sometimes my father and I would go out to dinner, and then he would drop me off at the mall. After that, I wouldn't see him for a few years; maybe it would be three to five years. Sometimes he would answer his phone, and sometimes he wouldn't. He chose the streets over his children! My father had four girls, me included; I was the oldest daughter on his side as well. After me, there was Brianna, Brooklyn, and little Shayla. I've never met Shayla, but one day I am sure I will. Brianna and I have a great relationship; likewise, I have a great relationship with Bria and De'Asia on my mother's side. I don't see or talk with Brooklyn much.

My father never really came into my life for a true genuine relationship until I was about nineteen. Although I went to live with his sister, my Aunt Pam, when I was seventeen, he was around more, but we still didn't have the best of relationships.

I believe one of the reasons I grew up with the perception of men that I had was because of the way my father treated me; I thought that way was right, that men were good only for material things—for having money to spend. Although he lied constantly, didn't show up, or otherwise let me down (that was a *major* feeling I had as a child: let down), I still loved him. It messed me up mentally because I grew up thinking that men had to spend money on me. I was very materialistic; that was all that I had known.

With my mother working all the time and being a single parent that needed someone to watch my sisters and me, she didn't really have *a lot* of help. I remember going to a place back in my hometown called the Job Center. This was a resource place for labor market exchange and workforce development. They provided assistance for almost anything. One day while in there, my mother saw a listing for a woman who had a babysitting service. My mother didn't know this woman, but because she had no help at the time and needed it, she took the babysitter's number off the big brown bulletin board. She called her and hired her.

I remember going over to the sitter's house for the first time. Her name was Ms. Paulette. Her house was big and nice. It was an off-white color, kind of like those houses you see in the older movies, where the houses were huge with expansive wooden floors and a big, wide front porch. She had a huge front yard with a big, beautiful green tree in the front. Walking up to the door, I could see she had an enclosed patio on the front end of the house.

I was nervous meeting Ms. Paulette for the first time. When she opened the door, I didn't make any attempt to greet her. I did not like leaving my mother's side, especially if it meant going to spend time with someone I didn't know. Due to my being in school, Ms. Paulette was not yet keeping me, only my two sisters.

We walked in and sat on the couch. I remember my first thought was that she was Chinese because her whole house was a China theme, from the bedroom to the kitchen. I was probably around eleven at the time, while De'Asia was probably five and Bria just a baby. Ms. Paulette had two sons and a daughter who stayed with her, and one other daughter who was grown with a son of her own. She also had a nephew that stayed in the basement; he had just gotten out of jail (I'm not sure my mother knew about that because I didn't even find out myself until months later.).

The first meeting with Ms. Paulette wasn't bad. About a week or two later, my sisters and I had begun going over to Ms. Paulette's every morning. My mother would drop us off early in the morning due to her early work schedule. De'Asia and I would then catch the bus to school, and after school our bus dropped us back off at her house.

Everything was OK for a while at first, but then things took a sudden turn. My mom sometimes would need the babysitter for work purposes, but other times she might have just wanted to have "Mommy time." After a while we started to stay at Ms. Paulette's a bit longer, and then started frequently staying the night. My sisters and I would sleep in the room with Ms. Paulette. She had her king-sized bed with the Chinese symbols on the comforter. At the foot of her bed was another bed—this one was twin-sized—on which my sisters and I slept when we stayed the night.

One time I woke up in the middle of the night and walked down Ms. Paulette's long wooden steps that led downstairs. The front door was open, and all the downstairs lights were on. Ms. Paulette was on the front patio, where she had great big wicker chairs that were painted white with tables to match. She had turned on the television, which was one of those old-school TVs with the big box on back, and it was sitting on the floor. I walked down the stairs and peeked around the corner to see where she was on the patio. I saw her asleep in the chair, her hand holding a forty-ounce beer. I must have moved too fast or bumped something, because I woke her up. She turned toward the door where I was standing and asked, "What are you doing?" It scared me and made me nervous because I already had a funny feeling about her. She looked a little scary, even, with really high cheek-bones, glossy yellowish eyes, and big teeth that weren't so white.

I replied, "I came to get some water, because I am thirsty." She then instructed me to "go into the kitchen, get you some water, and get back upstairs and into bed." I did what she asked and went back upstairs.

About this time, is when I started disliking the prospect of going over to Ms. Paulette's house. She had become slightly meaner and a little crazy. I started to notice her daily habit of drinking those big beers and smoking weed. She might even have had a mental illness. One morning after my sisters and I stayed the night, we woke up to Ms. Paulette's yelling at the top of her lungs at the TV. In fact, she was arguing with what one of the characters on the show was saying, as if she were part of that conversation. Crazy! While she was yelling, I could see vomit still on the side of her mouth. It was coming out of a corner of her mouth, trickling down the side of her jaw, past her chin and into a big puddle of vomit right on her shirt.

I assumed Ms. Paulette had been drinking all night. Every time she would drink excessively, she would wake up with vomit on her shirt. "Christopher, you love me, not that white tramp!!" she yelled at the TV. For whatever reason, Ms. Paulette believed she was in a relationship with Christopher. Is it any wonder I thought she was *crazy*!! She used to really talk about this TV character Christopher as if they were going to get married. She'd say things like, "He ran away to be on the show to get back at me after an argument we had," or "He will be back one day, he just needs space." Just down right *crazy*!!!

Her putting us to bed consisted of her telling my sisters and me to go to bed, then leaving to go downstairs to get high and drunk. Eventually, we just had to make ourselves fall asleep.

I had never seen anything like it in my eleven years, and it was creepy. It was a routine once she "put us to bed" or she thought she had put us to bed. Her putting us to bed consisted of her telling my sisters and me to go to bed, then leaving to go downstairs to get high and drunk. Eventually, we just had to make ourselves fall asleep. Ms. Paulette's oldest son, Levi, knew that was a ritual of hers. He knew once she made it downstairs, she would be down there for a few hours.

One night when Ms. Paulette was downstairs doing her usual thing, Levi came into the bedroom. I woke up and found him sitting beside me on the bed pinching both of my nostrils so that they were closed. I jumped up, only to be mugged back down by him balling up his fist and saying, "You better shut the fuck up and not say a thing!"

I was scared. Levi was seventeen and in high school at a school named Cornell White. I was only eleven. He was tall and skinny with braids that didn't hang past his ear. He had yellow teeth and a long narrow pointy nose. Seeing his face in my head even now makes me want to gag! Once he told me to shut up, he put one of his hands in my pants. I tried to fight him off, but that only resulted in my getting punched, slapped, or pinched! In my mind, I was defeated. At that moment, I thought back to the very first time I had walked downstairs and seen Ms. Paulette in her chair asleep. "What could she do to help me?" I thought as I laid there while Levi was touching me.

He and his mother fought all the time. He was *extremely* disrespectful to her. He would curse her out, call her names, threaten her, and sometimes do all the above, and she wouldn't do a thing to him. I figured she didn't have any power over Levi: he would hurt her and me.

So that night I lay there, and I took it. And as time went on, he continued to touch me and I allowed it. I started to know what was coming, and I was willing to let him pull my pants down and allow what he was doing to me. It went from his touching me to his inserting himself inside of me. I knew if I tried to fight him, he would hit me. I didn't want to get hit in my nose, eye, or anywhere for that matter, so I allowed it. I told my mother one morning when she was dropping us off at Ms. Paulette's house. I said to her, "I don't want to go over here." My mother's response was, "Well, you're going to have to go there because I have to work, and there's no one else helping me with you all."

I was so hurt. I didn't realize it at the time, but that situation along with a few other things built in me a lot of resentment toward my mother. I felt as if she should have known what I was going through. A mother knows, right!? I felt that she should have been able to tell by my voice. She should have asked me, "Why don't you want to go over there?" During this whole time, she never once asked me how we were being treated over there.

Ms. Paulette had a house full of people. My mom, however, never asked, "Do you like Ms. Paulette or her kids?" I guess back then it didn't matter. Mommy had to work, and we needed somewhere to go. Perhaps she was tied up with her own problems to even ask. Or maybe she just really didn't think she needed to ask because she was the parent. It took me a long time—a very long time, in fact—to realize that my mother was dealing with her own issues and living her own life, that she had worries of her own, and needed to deal with stuff in her life. This is not to say that my mother was uncaring for me, but she probably just didn't think to ask those questions.

Parenting doesn't come with an instruction manual, nor does it come with a rule book. You only know to do what you've been taught. What I do know is that she raised my sisters and me to the best of her ability. If she had known better back then, she would have done something about our situation with Ms. Paulette.

My sisters and I were under the care of Ms. Paulette for about a year to a year and a half. Eventually, my mother and she had a disagreement about a certain situation, and we stopped going over there. I was *extremely* happy when my mother said that we didn't have to go back over to Ms. Paulette's house anymore!!! There were a lot of things I didn't have to deal with anymore.

Looking back, my middle school years were depressing. I didn't know it at the time leading up to when I got to middle school and even high school that a lot of things I had gone through were taking their toll on me, affecting the way I acted or how I reacted to things. I was getting into more fights, just horrible fights. I stole things from stores or from a family member. I would steal or get into fights, then feel really bad right afterward. For just a few seconds it was like I didn't have control over what I was doing, whether it was stealing or fighting. As crazy as it sounds, I didn't even like fighting or stealing—it would just happen.

One of my teachers suggested to my mother that I go to counseling. So that's what my mother did to see if that would help me, or at least provide some answers as to what was going on with me. When my mother took me to the counselor, I remember crying as we were walking in, and thinking "I'm not crazy. Why do I have to go here? Nothing is wrong with me." It's not typical in African American communities for people to seek this kind of help when they need it! The common fear is that you'll be labeled as crazy. Or certain people might just think you're better off without it. Even when I got older, new issues arose. I spoke with my father about seeking help professionally, and he said he was all the counselor I needed. It's funny how people will reject the idea of seeking help when it is needed.

Truthfully, I needed it! I needed my mother in there with me, though. I wanted to talk to her and tell her what had been going on, but I just couldn't, or at least I didn't know how to.

Upon entering the room, I saw that the counselor was a black woman with short hair. She had on red lipstick and was wearing a tan skirt suit. When I got inside the room, she told me, "OK, you can talk to me. Tell me anything you want me to know, and it will be between you and me." As she was saying this to me, she pulled out a tape recorder and hit record.

I'd never been through this before and didn't know what

the protocol was for a session with a counselor, but all I could think was that she was recording this conversation so she could replay it for my mom. Certainly, I had mixed feelings about this whole situation. I wanted my mom to know, but then again, I didn't. I wanted her to be in the room with me, but then again, I didn't. I wanted her to know because maybe then she would pay more attention to me once knowing what was going on with me. I felt like, "OK, if she knows this, then maybe that will be a wakeup call for her to pay more attention to me and for us to build a greater relationship." I wanted her to be in the room because maybe, *just maybe*, that counselor could get us both in on a session and we just talk *everything* out and come to a resolution and my mother's relationship with me would get better, like in the movies. Unfortunately, that didn't happen.

I didn't feel as if my mother liked me for a long time just because of the way that she acted toward me. Things that I witnessed—like her *always* being on the phone with her friends, talking about all the bad things I had done had tremendously lower my self-esteem. I'll be the first to say I was not innocent by any stretch! But hearing certain things after you continually tried to do better made it like, What's the point?! I spent a whole childhood trying to be perfect for someone who I thought never appreciated me or saw the good in me.

3

Dysfunctionally Functional

ALL AROUND THE WORLD THERE ARE PEOPLE OF DIFFERENT ethnic backgrounds and ages struggling with some form of abnormal and/or unhealthy behavior. We normalize deviant behavior and tend to become a product of our environment by thinking the wrong things that we are engaging in are right. We tend to make excuses for certain things that we do because we've seen it done for so long that we just "go with the flow." We say things like. . . . "Well, Daddy, Mama, Grandpa, and friends older than me have slept with married men/women, and, to the naked eye, it looks like they don't have to deal with consequences or repercussions, so I could do it, too, and be just fine!"

Many people have experienced dry humping as a child, mainly female to female or male to female, and they've just grown up and now seem to be just fine. Almost everyone has had that older family member who has allowed them to smoke and drink before they were legally old enough to partake. Many people have been in abusive relationships, be it mentally or physically, and eventually they get through it. You'll hear things like "You may be in a storm for a while, but sooner or later the man will realize what a good thing he has." This logic is horrible. We must come out of this bad way of thinking. Until we do, nothing will ever be right.

Between the way things were for me at home, not doing well at school, and feeling like my whole world was shattering into pieces, I had fallen into a really bad state of depression. Maw-Maw had gotten sick; cancer had struck her body. She would constantly ask me to come and visit while she was in the hospital. By the time I finally got to see her, her sickness had gotten much worse. She soon passed way, and I was devastated.

As my feelings toward myself—my self-esteem—continued to decline, I became suicidal. I felt like I had the weight of the world on my shoulders. I would go into my closet (that was my hiding spot) and, literally, pray and ask God to take me away. At such a young age, I can remember sitting on a basketful of clothes in the closet asking God, "Why did you create me?! Why don't you just take me away, I don't want to be here anymore!!!" I would say all this in such an angry voice, trying to wish myself away.

My mother tried everything. She would ground me, take things away, even send me to church with *everyone*!!! That meant even going to church with my aunt, who is a Jehovah's Witness. I went everywhere. I dealt with a lot. I felt like I was the parent in a lot of situations.

The alarm clock was always in my room. I would always have to be the one to set it every night, and then I would be the first one up in the morning. I would go wake up my mother, and then go wake up my sisters. I would have to iron my mother's clothes and my sisters' clothes. On top of that, I was always having to keep the house clean, including my sisters' room and closet. That didn't sit well with me; like I said, I felt as if I were the parent.

There were times when my mother would go out and have a good time at night. The next day my sisters and I would have to go to school, and I would wake up looking for my mother. She would be nowhere in the house. One day the next-door neighbor called me and told me that my mother was outside and that I needed to come and get her. I opened the door and there she was, asleep in the car. That happened on many occasions. Before I woke up my sisters, I would go outside and get Mom out of the car and help her into the house. I just thank God that she always made it home safely with no accidents or DUIs.

Trying to commit suicide was my cry for help. I didn't want to leave this world; I just wanted the pain to stop. I didn't want my heart to hurt anymore, and, honestly, I just wanted my mommy.

I held a lot of things in, but those times helping my mom like that, along with everything else, led up to a breaking point for me. I felt like really didn't have a childhood; it was taken away from me in many forms. In the same breath, I also must say I really did want to live; I just didn't want to live the way that I had been living. I needed help, and I wanted help.

Trying to commit suicide was my cry for help. I didn't want to leave this world; I just wanted the pain to stop. I didn't want my heart to hurt anymore, and, honestly, I just wanted my mommy. I tried to commit suicide once. It was on a day when my mother wasn't home, but I was with my little sister De 'Asia. I was so down emotionally. I had been getting yelled at all day for not cleaning the house and some other things, and I had just had it. I remember telling my sister that I was going to run away. Ha, I had never done that or even tried. I always thought to myself, "Man, when your mama finds you, she's going to kill you!" I told my sister that was what I was going to do.

I thought about that—running away—for a while, but as time went on, I felt my heart getting heavier and heavier. I got a knife and put it to my wrist, and I told my sister that I was about to just kill myself. *"Shay! No!!!!!!!!* Then what are we going to do?! Who's going to watch after me and Bria!" my baby sister yelled out with tears in her eyes. It was at that moment that I knew I had a purpose, although I didn't exactly know what it was. All I needed to know was that someone truly loved me. I had just wanted to be loved.

To this day I still yearn for my mother's love, affection, and deep relationship. At that time, De'Asia's love was enough to keep me alive—for me to put the knife away. That's who I did it for—for her and Bria. They became who I lived for. I never tried to commit suicide again. They still got on my nerves, though; we fought at times, and we still argue and fight because that's what sisters do. If it wasn't for them, I'm not sure where I would be today.

My relationship with my mother was still not in a good place. As I got older, I had grown to resent her more and more. I loved her, but we did not get along. My deepest desire was for us to get along, but we just did not click. I grew up feeling like she didn't like me, like she hated me, and her actions didn't make me feel any different. Most of those feelings could have been prevented had I just been open with her and expressed to her what had gone on, but I just didn't feel like my mother was approachable, I didn't feel like I could go to her with a problem and that she would help me solve it. She was so head strong, so stubborn.

If you didn't agree with what she thought was right, it was an issue to her. So, I began to keep everything to myself. I did finally tell her what the babysitter's son had done to me when I was a sophomore in high school. Once I finally told her, nothing happened. It was just me telling her, then her asking me why I hadn't told her at the time, then me voicing to her that I was scared, and then that was the end of the discussion.

More should have been done. I didn't feel comforted. I believed my mother should have gone and had a talk with Ms. Paulette and her son. The authorities should have been contacted. I mean, *something*! At the time, I thought I had let it go, but I had done nothing but swallow the pain and allowed it—along with everything else I had encountered—allowed it to build up.

When I first started my menstrual cycle, it was very irregular. There was a hormonal imbalance, which I didn't find out about until I was nineteen. Because my cycle was irregular, sometimes I would come on, and other times I would skip a month or two. My mother started to notice. I remember a few times where she had me urinate into a cup and place it under the sink in the bathroom. I'd get up the next day, and use the restroom and peek under the counter to see if the cup was still there, but it would be gone.

I had no clue why she had me doing that, until one day when I went snooping in her room (which I did frequently). Being the oldest girl, or I should say just being a girl, period, I always went into my mother's room and went through things to see what I could take and wear to school, whether it be lotion, jewelry, knee highs, stockings, purses, *anything*. One day while in there, I found a box of pregnancy tests. It then dawned on me that that's why she needed me to urinate in the cup; she was giving me tests to see if I was pregnant. Seeing that hurt me the most. It hurt me because at the time I wasn't even sexually active. My biggest feeling of resentment was, "Well, she gave me the test, and she found out that I wasn't pregnant, so what's next?" She never took me to the doctor to see why my cycle was irregular. She just kept giving me the test, and once she got her result, that was that.

That pissed me off. As I think back now, I believe what I was experiencing at that point was hurt, although at the time it felt more like anger. Time had passed, and I had grown older. I was now fifteen or sixteen, still helping Mom with my sisters, who had gotten older and could take care of themselves more. Not everything was horrible, but I still was searching for approval. My mother still wasn't there for me—emotionally. I also felt alone, and I was extremely vulnerable.

My mom entertained *lots* of people. She was the life of the party. She was a people person and had a lot of friends—people she knew either from having worked with them or grown up with them. Dayton is a small city. I still believe my mother knows half, if not all, the city.

One time in particular, she had company over to the house—a guy by the name of DeWayne. DeWayne was someone I believe my mother had dated when she was younger. He was a barber. When I first met him, I didn't like him. His eyes told it all. There was just something about him that I did not agree with. I believed he was extremely sneaky, a snake!

On this occasion that DeWayne was over, my mother had cooked and he was sitting at the dinner table. My mother had gone to the back of the room for something. DeWayne called me over to the table and told me that I should come to the shop sometime for him to do my eyebrows. He then took both of his hands and felt both of my eyebrows, before moving his hands down my face, caressing it on both sides. My heart dropped. I was scared and annoyed. I pulled away my face from his hands and went into my bedroom.

Let me backtrack a bit to before that face-caressing encounter. Earlier, I had been walking in the hallway with a new

Blackberry phone that my father had sent me in the mail. De-Wayne had seen me on the phone using the Internet. He asked to see my phone, because it was the newest Blackberry. At first, he seemed interested in checking out the phone, but quickly it came to me that he was just trying to be slick and figure out a way to get my number, which is exactly what he did. The whole time he had my phone, he was texting himself to get my phone number. I didn't realize he had done this until he left and later texted me, saying only, "Hey." I didn't know who it was, so I replied, "Who is this?!" Of course, it was DeWayne! I instantly told him to stop texting my phone or I was going to let my mother know. I erased his number and ignored the next messages he sent!

A few months later, I found out that DeWayne's kids went to the same after-school program that my sisters and I attended. I saw him one day there as I was walking past the front desk, and he grabbed me and hugged me. As he did that, he kissed me on my neck. I walked away in disgust. I never told my mom about this ordeal because I just didn't have any faith that, one, she would believe me, and two, that she would do anything about it.

Another guy that she dated would come to the house and made lots of passes at me. This guy had gone to jail for drugs; he also was known for messing with younger females my age. I remember being at school one day and telling my friend—who was his niece—about him saying things to me that were out of line. One of the security guards at the school overheard our conversation, and he went and told the principal. The next day the principal called me into her office and asked me about the situation. Prior to this meeting with the principal, I didn't know that this man had had previous issues, to include being in trouble with the law for statutory rape. It was during my conversation with the principal that I found out all this stuff. She told me that she would have to tell my mother, which I didn't want her to do, but she had to—he wasn't supposed to be around kids or schools.

Later that evening my mother called me and asked, "Why is the principal calling me to tell me that James was trying to talk to you?"

I said, "Because the security guard overheard a conversation and went and told her."

It turns out the security guard had known this man and the many questionable or illegal acts he had done. He knew he wasn't allowed to be within so many feet of a school, etc. so he, the security guard, was basically looking out for my safety, although at the time I was mad about it, thinking he was just being nosy, getting into my business.

He, the security guard, was basically looking out for my safety, although at the time I was mad about it, thinking he was just being nosy, getting into my business.

Once I got off the phone with my mother, that was the end of that topic. A little while later, I was with my friend—the same one who's the niece with whom I had been having the overheard conversation—and my friend, her mom, and I were having a conversation about the situation concerning James. My friend's mom was really close with my mother. My mother has known them both since she was in kindergarten, and they all grew up together. This lady—my friend's mother—told me in the car that my mother told her that I might have egged on the situation with James, my friend's uncle, and that he probably didn't do all of what I said he had.

This was getting intolerable, and all it did for me was to put up another barrier, this time toward her; I knew she was never going to believe me, either. When I confronted my mom about what my friend's mother had just said to me, all my mother said back to me was that she knew what she had done, and that's when I knew I didn't have a chance with her.

My mother and I were, and are, two different people. I spent a lot of my time trying to convince her of something I wasn't, but what I didn't realize was that the words that were spoken over or at me accurately portrayed what I was slowly becoming, basically a flirt, egging things on, etc.

We had an extended family. One of the members of that extended family was Connie, a lady who lived down the street from my grandmother. My mother grew up calling her Momma. My sisters and I grew up calling her Granny. Connie had thirteen kids—nine boys and four girls. My sisters and I were close to two of the sisters, Renay and TeLeah. TeLeah was the oldest; Renay, with whom I was and still am really close to, was the younger of those two.

My sisters and I used to go over to each of their houses when we were growing up. That was one thing I really enjoyed about growing up—going over to see them. It was fun. I was always the oldest and was in charge because I was the babysitter. It was also freedom for me, so I didn't mind going over there. I was sixteen, and it was the summer before my senior year of high school.

There was one time when I was with TeLeah when we had just come from a funeral. TeLeah's brother, Gerald, owns a submarine sandwich shop, a food place best known for its cheesesteak sandwiches. We went up there for her to go and get some weed from her nephew Brandon, who worked at the sub shop. When we walked in and went behind the counter, I remember walking past Brandon and his saying to me, "Damn, girl, you smell good." I said, "Thanks," and that was the only encounter Brandon and I had, at least for the moment.

TeLeah got what she needed from Brandon and then we got in the car.

"Shay, Brandon wants your number," TeLeah said to me.

"What?!"

"Yeah, girl, you should talk to him, and he will buy you whatever you want and need."

I wasn't feeling too good about it, but I didn't care. I ignored those feelings. I didn't care that Brandon was thirty-one and I was sixteen. I didn't care or think about the fact that TeLeah was a good fourteen maybe fifteen years older than me. She should have known better than to set up a booty call (let's be real; that's what it was) between me and her nephew. I didn't care that he didn't want a relationship with me and that he just wanted my body. All that mattered to me at the time was that he wanted me. Someone wanted me, and I'd be lying if I sat here and acted completely innocent and said that I didn't have lustful eyes! I thought he was attractive. So, I told TeLeah she could give him my number.

Brandon texted my phone within no time and tried to have a short convo, but he ended up asking if he could see me later. I responded saying, "Yes!" My assumption was that he knew I was staying over at her house that evening, and I'm sure they had a conversation, which is why she came to me telling me he was interested. Brandon and I had a conversation over text messages that whole day.

That night, prior to Brandon's arrival at TeLeah's house, I was *extremely* nervous. I was so scared because of his age, and I had never willingly had sex, so I wasn't experienced at all. I was thinking the whole time, "What have I gotten myself into?!" I wanted so badly to seem grown up, so I began getting myself ready. I took a shower and sprayed on so much perfume that I was covered all over my neck and on down to my toes!

There was a knock on the door, and there he was, dressed in an orange, blue, yellow, and green polo button up, with blue jeans and an orange hat. He had a red cup in his hand that he took a sip from as I was opening the door. Once I opened the door, he kissed me in my mouth like I had never been kissed before. It was passionate, sensual; he made me feel wanted. In the back of my mind I was still a bit scared, but I didn't care. He kissed me from the front room to the back room, which was TeLeah's room. We closed the door, and he began to undress me, taking off my pants first. He kissed me all over my neck then kissed me in my mouth, and I could taste all the alcohol in the perfume that I sprayed on my neck due to my nervousness. He proceeded to perform oral sex on me.

At that moment, I wanted to call the whole thing off. It hurt bad. That was something I just wasn't used to, and he was not gentle at all. Still, I didn't stop him. I continued to allow him to do what he wanted to do. Once we were finished, I was in disbelief that I had just done what I had done, and I felt very weird. We laid there in the bed for a while, and he looked deep into my eyes in what I thought back then was a weird way.

He rubbed me from the top of my head down the side of my face as he was looking into my eyes and telling me "You're so beautiful" and "I really like you." I didn't like him like that, though, so to me that was weird. I just responded with, "No, you don't." I didn't believe him for several reasons; one main reason being that he was a whole fifteen years older than me. I didn't know at the time what I was opening myself up to, but I soon found out. From that day forward, Brandon called me *every day*! He would call from work, home, when he was out. . . . He called all the time. Sometimes I would answer and other times I wouldn't. The times that I did answer and we would talk, the conversation wouldn't be about anything but him always telling me how he loved me. He would call me and vent to me about his problems for the day, and I would just listen.

After that first time of our having intercourse, he would always try to get another chance at going at it again, but it never transpired. We only had sex that one time, and that was it. For years he tried and tried again. I just knew it was wrong the first time and never went back. Eventually, after all the calls and texts throughout the day, I told him that he would have to stop. Brandon stated that he respected my decision, and that was the last I spoke to him on that level of our being more than mere acquaintances.

Part II: Self-Inflicted Pain

4
Falling in Lust

I ONCE READ IN A BLOG BY PEACE QUARTERS THAT "WE ONLY fall in love with three people in our lifetime—each one for a specific reason." (www.peacequarters.com)

The first love, the blog states, happens when we're young, perhaps in our teen years. This first love is defined as one that fulfills the dreams of our youth and the idealistic belief of what we expect love to look like. We jump into this love with enthusiasm, believing that this person will be our only love (even if it doesn't feel quite right) and convince ourselves that this is how love should look.

The second love is what Peace Quarters refers to as the "hard love." This love teaches us lessons about ourselves and what we need in order to feel loved in any relationship. However, this love is accompanied by *great pain*—the pain of loss, deceit, and lies. It is with this love that we believe we are doing things differently, but actually we are not (Ha! That was me). Typically, we tend to persevere in holding on to this love because this relationship is different from the first one. It is through this second love where we come to understand what we really need out of our next relationship. This love tends to become cyclical—repeating the same issues over and over, each time expecting a different result.

This love is often unhealthy and rather unbalanced. During this love, there can be emotional or physical abuse, and often there is some form of manipulation at play. This love is surrounded by a constant state of drama—it becomes addictive and it's difficult to break the cycle.

The third love is the love that comes out of left field. It surprises us and goes against what we envisioned our love should look like! This love is easy; it is uncomplicated and not filled with expectations. This love does not look like the love we dreamed we would have, and it does not adhere to any of the rules we had set for ourselves. This love just simply feels right. It is the love that teaches us how to feel love and how to give love.

You might find that you only have one love during your lifetime. Your journey to that third love is not identical to any other person's journey. Only you will be able to experience your love story. No matter where you are in the cycle of love—the ideal love, the broken love, or the perfect love—you will find that you can learn something in each love.

I can honestly say that I've experienced the first two loves or what I thought to be love for sure!! In each of the particular relationships that I am about to describe concerning love, I had warning signs that things weren't right. We all do! Every woman has warning signs in relationships; we just choose to do one of the following:

A) Ignore the warning signs for several reasons. This could be because of the fear of the unknown—of what's on the other side. You suffer from a low self-esteem; maybe you don't think you'll get any better than what you have.

B) We are blind to the warning signs. We are clueless to

what's going on because we come from a long line of dysfunction. We normalize the abnormal.

C) We remain hoping that they'll change. After all, Beyoncé said it best in her song "On the Run (Part II)": "Who wants that perfect love story anyway, cliché, cliché, cliché, cliché. Who wants that hero love that saves the day? What about that bad guy goes good?!"

We all want a love like that, right? I know I did. I wanted that bad guy that went good. I wanted to help change him. This is the guy to whom you give your pleasure in exchange for their pain. For me, it all started in the beginning of my senior year of high school. This was when I met the "ideal love." I was sixteen about to turn seventeen. I had a friend by the name of Sharde. She and I were extremely close. We always had done everything together. I didn't have a boyfriend and hadn't had one at all. Sharde dated a guy named Robert. He had a cousin by the name of Eric.

Sharde and I were on the school bus one morning headed to school, and she said to me, "Robert's cousin wants to talk to you." I didn't know who Robert's cousin was, nor did I know anything about him. So, she showed me a picture of him from his MySpace page. He was a tall, darker-brown-skinned guy with a red hat on turned toward the back. In his mouth was a top and bottom gold grill that I saw, as he had a grin that went from ear to ear, his face was on the rougher side. He was holding a big stack of money up by his right cheek. I gravitated right toward him. I told Sharde that she could give him my number when she saw him.

Eric was always at his cousin Robert's house, and back then Sharde was always there over as well. We set up a double date. Sharde, Robert, Eric, and I all went to Steak and Shake, where we had a great time, just sitting around and joking, as kids do. Eric and Robert were both older than Sharde and me; they were both out of high school. Eric was nineteen. I also found out that night while we were out that he had a kid who was two years old. I still liked him, though, a lot, after that first encounter.

He was funny, cool, and very interesting, plus he had this roughness about him, and for whatever reason I had always been attracted to those type of guys. I always wanted the ones who were in the streets, the thugs, the roughnecks. I wanted someone who could "handle me." Deep down, I didn't realize that I was soul searching. I didn't realize I was looking for my father in every man I came across. What I didn't realize was that for the next seven years, I would actually be looking for a counselor under the covers!

That date at Steak and Shake set things in motion for Eric and me. That night I went back to Robert's house with Sharde. Sharde was staying the night with Robert, so, me being careless, I decided to stay with Eric downstairs. We laid there the whole night. We kissed a little and touched a little, but no sex! I didn't want to give it up that fast, and I didn't know him all that well.

After that night, Eric and I grew closer and closer. I remember him coming over to my house all the time. It was young "love" or what I thought was love. I guess it was love. Eric was my first boyfriend and he treated me so good. In the beginning, we didn't have any issues. He had become a good friend of mine. I started to fall for him expeditiously!!

It was going on our fifth month of dating, and Eric and I were spending a lot of time together. I knew he already had a kid, and that he was older, and that I liked him a lot and wanted to have sex with him. At the same time, I wanted to stay safe and protect myself, so for weeks I prepared a speech

56

on how I was going to ask my mother to put me on birth control. The perfect day to bring it up with her never happened, so one day I just went for it. I walked out of my room and heard her in the kitchen fixing something to eat for all of us. I walked up to the counter.

"Mom, can you put me on birth control?!"

"Birth control for what?!" she responded.

"Well, you know, I'm with Eric. I really like him, and he already has a kid, I just want to be safe." That was my reply.

My mother just walked off and went into her room and closed the door. No response. No looking at me in the face, nothing. I didn't know how to feel in that moment. All I knew was that I was still determined to get on birth control because I didn't know what could or would happen, and I did just that. The next day I made an appointment to go to Planned Parenthood. I then called one of my aunts and asked her if she could give me a ride, which she did.

Maybe my mother just didn't know how to deal with it at the time. Perhaps she was shocked that she just had discovered that I either was sexually active or about to become sexually active. That wall between her and me that had been building for several years had just gotten even higher.

Once I was on birth control, Eric and I became sexually active. It wasn't until I got older that I found out that when you're having sex with someone outside of whom God has designed for you to be with, things get really tricky. Your vision gets cloudy and your judgment goes awry. My mother and I were feuding more and more, and Eric was my go-to person. He was always there for me. When my mother and I had an argument or disagreement, I would take all those feelings and run to Eric, who was always one phone call away. He was sweet, considerate, understanding—he was that person who always answered.

My mother knew he and I were getting closer and closer, so if she and I were having a fight and I needed something later that evening (such as eczema cream, sanitary napkins, food, my phone bill paid, etc.), she would tell me, "Why don't you have him do it!" So, I did just that, and I started to ask him for everything. He began paying my cellphone bill, giving me rides where I needed or wanted to go. He was always there. I ran into his arms.

My mind had become so wrapped around him that I was falling in lust and not in love. He was who I desired; I felt I needed him to survive. While I was living at home, he took my mind off the pain that I dealt with. Back then I didn't even have a label for what I was feeling. I just knew when I was around him I didn't think about the drama of my mother and me, or the responsibility of watching my sisters, or making sure the house was clean. Time had gone on and Eric knew how I felt and what was going on at my mother's house.

He began to influence me to get pregnant by him. He begged and pleaded that I stop taking the birth control that I was taking and that I become pregnant. His words were, "You know you can leave her house, so what if you're only seventeen?! If you get pregnant, you could leave and the government could give you a place. You'll be good; you don't need her!" Eric never tried to help me resolve the situation, though. He soon became the problem and encouraged a lot of my disobedience toward my mother. I longed for a great relationship with my mom, but he didn't care about that. Although I wanted a good relationship with her, I wasn't going about it the right way, and soon I began to forget about wanting that great relationship.

Eric had a lot of influence with me. I wanted to get out of my mother's house, and I didn't care how I did it. Eric and I began to start having unprotected sex—a *big no-no*! I tried and tried to get pregnant by him. I even prayed to God, "Lord please allow me to get pregnant so that I can leave this place!" *Man*!!! I am so glad that God never answered that prayer. Nor did he answer the prayers I spoke about in chapter 2, where I asked God to just take me away, when I didn't want to live. Although I was off and on with the birth control I was using, I never got pregnant during the three years Eric and I were together. Thank God for unanswered prayers.

Eric and I would argue and he would talk as if he was all that I had. He had become possessive and controlling. I allowed it; after all, he was the one who looked out for me the most when I needed it.

Eric and I would argue and he would talk as if he was all that I had. He had become possessive and controlling. I allowed it; after all, he was the one who looked out for me the most when I needed it. I started to rebel even harder against my mother because of the influence that I was under. I began sneaking Eric into our house, sneaking over to his place, just all types of crazy things just to be with him. And when my mother wouldn't allow me to see him or go and be with him, I would still try to find a way. I convinced myself I needed to be with him, I needed to see him.

It was in May 2010 that my mother decided she was going to move to Nashville, Tennessee. I had just graduated high school and would be eighteen that following September. My mother was going to move in August, and when she told me that, I knew I did not want to go. I was in a relationship with Eric. Plus, all my friends were there in Dayton, and I just knew that if my mom and I didn't get along in Ohio, then we definitely wouldn't be getting along in Nashville.

My mother went for one weekend to check out Nashville and to search for a place, and by the time she came back, she had found a house. I was happy for her, but I was also worried thinking she would make me go with her. She didn't, however. This came during a season where my father and I were "on," getting along, and the plan was for me to move in with him. He made all these promises that I could come and live with him, telling me how that was something that he'd always wanted for me, and I believed him.

When it came time for my mother to leave for Tennessee, I didn't hear from my father. I was determined to stay in Ohio, so I desperately sought out my grandparents—my mother's parents. I called my grandmother, asking her if I could come stay with them. My grandmother, knowing the condition of the relationship between my mother and me, opened her home to me.

With that settled, Eric and I took that road trip with my mother to help her move and unpack. I could tell when I was saying good-bye to my mother before I headed back to Dayton that she wasn't happy about me not coming to Nashville with her to live. Something I've learned as I've grown older is that people can feel a certain way about something, but pride will be standing in the way. Maybe they want to tell you something, but because of pride or because of an assumption about how they think you'll react, they won't say it. My mother is a very headstrong person and, in some cases, she can come off as "emotionless." At least that's how I saw it growing up. Although she might not have wanted me to leave her, she allowed me to anyway and didn't say a word.

I later found out that she didn't want me to go and that she didn't like Eric. She didn't like him because of the way he expressed his attitude toward me and the way he had become toward her. His attitude toward me was terrible, and he talked crazy. I was going to miss my sisters. I loved them, but I knew they would be OK. It was indeed hard leaving them at first, but we had a great long talk and they understood.

Once my mother had moved, I went and stayed with my grandparents, which was cool and peaceful, although my stay with them wasn't for long. In the short amount of time I ended up staying there, I grew to dislike it. My grandmother protected me as if I were still her little girl. That meant I couldn't really go with Eric when and where I wanted, and I always had to be back by a certain time. Being the rebellious child I was, I wanted to do my own thing and have a sense of freedom. Once I turned eighteen, I told my grandmother that I was going to move in with my Aunt Diane, who had a major role in my sisters' lives as well as mine. She helped my mother raise us. We spent most of our childhood with her as well as her mother and her sisters. Blood couldn't make us any closer. I knew that I could always go to Diane for anything I needed. She knew all about my mother's relationship with me, and she was there a lot for me when I was younger, whether it was just for me to vent or if I needed to get away; she was there for me.

Aunt Diane helped me to believe in myself growing up. She was my confidante. I remember battling with self-esteem issues growing up; I used to tell her how I felt ugly. One day in particular, she made me grab a mirror and look in it and tell myself, "I am beautiful. I am smart. I am strong." I repeated those words until I believed them.

Staying with her wasn't bad. She allowed me to have my freedom, and I liked that, although it was both a good thing and a bad thing. Eric and I continued with our relationship, which was going on three years now.

One night I had a dream that I was pregnant, and Eric and I were fighting. Somehow, in the dream, I ended up on the ground, where Eric began kicking me in the stomach. When I woke up, I felt as if I had just experienced the weirdest thing in the world. I didn't realize at the time that God was, in a way, showing me what was about to happen. A few months later, Eric went from being possessive and controlling to being physically abusive. We would always have arguments about the silliest things. It went from him grabbing me and throwing me up against a wall to more aggressive things, like punches in the face.

At first, we would fight, and I thought it was cute—like the roughing-me-up part. He started that one day when he saw a guy inbox me on Facebook. He always went through my phone, but I never erased anything; I didn't have a reason to. Once he saw that Facebook message, he instantly came charging toward me, grabbed me by the collar of my shirt, and pushed me up against his aunt's brick fireplace in her living room, asking me, "Are you fucking him!?"

I was shocked. I couldn't believe he was blowing up in such a manner. That wasn't all. If someone commented under my picture and I commented back, he got mad. He didn't want me commenting. Any of my male friends that I had, I couldn't have them anymore because he didn't want me to. Eric was so controlling. He was jealous of the thought of me with another guy. In a way I was scared, but in another way, I felt protected at the time.

Quite frankly, that sort of behavior boils down to manipulation. It's almost as if he were trying to scare me into staying with him and not talking to anyone but him—to not think about or deal with anyone but him. Sadly, that had become my new reality. I had gotten used to the abuse.

One evening we were out driving and he was dropping me off at my aunt's house. Eric at the time lived with his grandmother. I'm not sure what it was about, but all I know is that as he was dropping me off, we were arguing. The next thing I know, he reached over and punched me in the nose! All I could feel was hurt, disgust, and disbelief! I couldn't believe that this was the way that I was living. Tears flowed down my face, but Eric didn't say a word. No apology, no affection, no sympathy.

I got out of the car with a bloody nose and didn't say anything as I slammed the truck door and ran up the stairs. He quickly jumped out of the truck in an attempt to stop me from running up to the top level, where my aunt's apartment was. "*Come back here!*" he yelled. Eric didn't care about the neighbors or my aunt, for that matter.

"I have to get something for my nose!!" I yelled back at him in a shaky, distraught voice— it was hard for me to speak because of how hard I was crying. Thankfully, my aunt wasn't home when I got there. She was at work.

"I have to get something for my nose!!" I yelled back at him in a shaky, distraught voice—it was hard for me to speak because of how hard I was crying. Thankfully, my aunt wasn't home when I got there.

No one knew what I was going through with Eric until we ended our relationship for good. So, of course, I got something to stop and clean up my nosebleed, and then went back down the stairs. I should have been done with him at that moment, but I wasn't. He apologized, and I forgave him. He didn't punch me in the nose ever again, but the other forms of abuse continued.

Eric and I were off and on for the next two years. Our split wasn't easy. Eric used to always tell me if I left him he would kill himself, and he didn't have anything to live for. Although he had a kid, his mom, a sister and brother, and a host of family and extended family that loved him, he played on my emotions, telling me he had nothing to live for. He actually tried committing suicide because I was leaving him. That act landed him in a seventy-two-hour psych hold in a hospital. He called me asking me to come and see him in the hospital on those days, but I felt so uncomfortable I never did. His mother also suggested to me that I not visit him there.

After going through all of that with him, I still wasn't done. He got out of the hospital and we went maybe a week or two without talking, but shortly after things went right back. He was what I like to call "drama-fied"—he fed off drama. Although I had been in a lot of trouble as a kid because of my fighting, I wasn't a person full of drama. Half of the time I was fighting, it was due to being picked on, not anything I initiated.

To this day, I believe that Eric might have been involved with his child's mother some of the time that he and I were together. She and I had a few issues from the time she found out he was in a relationship and I had come fully into the picture. She didn't like the fact that he was in a relationship with someone else, and that I was younger than her. The mother of Eric's child was extremely childlike, and I fed right into her games. Somehow, she had gotten my phone number. She began playing games, calling my phone and making threats, so eventually she and I got into a fight. Here I was nineteen years old, not even in a relationship with Eric at the time (we had broken up, although we later got back together), fighting in the middle of the street over, as it appeared, a man.

After the fight was over, I was so embarrassed. A different side of me had been exposed. I had tried to hit the girl with my car; the police were called and a case was filed against me. At that moment, I didn't believe Eric had set up that fight, but I later found out that he had. Our relationship was so unstable and had so much chaos, it was just draining. I started to keep my distance from Eric, and we didn't talk for a while. During the off season of ours, I never was just fully single. I always had someone that I was involved with. And those guys that I dated were all in the streets. I had begun to just not care about men and started to do them how I had been done in my relationship. Wrong move!

I had become promiscuous and just made a lot of silly decisions. For the previous six months, my mother had been trying to convince me—and get others to help her convince me—to move to Nashville.

Soon after the fight, a close guy friend of mine got robbed and shot fifteen times, which led to his death. My mother begged me to come and move to Nashville with her. So many of my people were dying and going to jail; moving to Nashville was probably the best thing to do.

At first, I was so hesitant about moving for a number of reasons. First, I didn't want to move because of the not-so-ideal relationship I had with my mother. Second, I didn't want to move because Eric and I were off and on. I still loved him, and I wasn't ready to leave him yet. Everything had begun to fall apart in Ohio, though. I had lost my job as a receptionist at a youth career services organization, my car had gotten taken, and my relationship with Eric was in crumbles. All signs pointed to Nashville; I just wasn't hearing it.

I left kicking and screaming. I had no idea what God was up to, and little did I know that the fun was just about to begin.

5
Divine Intervention

Genesis 12:1
"Now the Lord said to Abram, 'Go from your country, your people and your father's house hold to the land that I will show you.'"

Divine Intervention – God's way of intervening in your life through human affairs.

Intervention – An act that alters the cause of a disease, injury, or condition by initiating a treatment or performing a procedure or surgery. (Webster's *definition*)

I FINALLY KICKED THE NEGATIVE THINKING WHEN IT CAME TO moving to Nashville. My mother was ready for me to come home to be with her. I called her and told her that I would come live with her, and she welcomed me with open arms!!

I had no idea that I was about to enter a whole new dimension that involved not only getting to know God but also getting to know who I was. The next five years would be a season full of tests, trials, and errors for me. It would be a period when I would be on the operating table, so to speak, undergoing a spiritual form of open-heart surgery. One great thing about undergoing this spiritual surgery was my father's return into my life. He never was truly there for me when I was a kid, but during this period, he was there for me like never before. This would be one of the seasons when I needed him most— which I'll talk more about later—and he was there, literally, through the whole process! Through my entire promiscuous phase, rebellious phase, etc.

Based on my own experiences, I can clearly see how God is so intentional in the things that he does.

Based on my own experiences, I can clearly see how God is so intentional in the things that he does. I was seventeen when my father and I started to build a true relationship—I was now old enough to know I needed his voice and that it mattered, as opposed to me thinking, "Well, he has never been there for me, so what type of advice could he possibly have for me?"

I moved to Nashville two weeks before my twentieth birthday. Within the first three weeks of being in Nashville, I found a job working at Buckle, a store best known for its sale of denim goods, in Rivergate Mall. Buckle was a great place to work, and it was where I met my first friend in Nashville— Rodney.

To this day, I truly believe that God set this whole friendship up! At work, I would always hear Rodney singing gospel songs. There was no shame in his game; he was loud and had the voice that would send chills through your body. One day, without hesitation, I asked him, "What church do you go to?" because I knew he had to be going somewhere. He replied, "Mount Zion."

Even before he said that, I knew I needed to find a home

church. I had never had one growing up. My mother would allow us as kids to go and visit churches with family/friends, and we would also go to vacation Bible school every summer. However, we never ended up belonging to a church that we would go to every Sunday. I knew at the time that Mom desired to join one, because we tried a few. I guess she just never found one that sat right with her.

When Rodney told me where he went to church, I instantly wanted to go visit it. Later that day, Rodney invited me to go with him to a Wednesday night Bible study, which I did, and I have been hooked ever since.

That was in October 2011. My first visit to Mount Zion was amazing. I continued to go every Sunday and Wednesday for the rest of the year. I joined the church at the New Year Eve's service, going into the year 2012.

I didn't have a car then, which is one of the reasons why I believe that God set up the friendship between Rodney and me. Every Sunday and Wednesday, he would come and get my sisters and me, and he would take us to church. Every week, two days out of the week, he was there. This continued for well over a year. I believe God used him in that time to ensure that I was getting back and forth to church, because he needed to build me up for all that was coming my way soon. All the tests that were coming to me were designed to break me, and I needed to get built up to be able to stand and not fall during those trials. I needed that word, it was my life. I wrapped myself around it as much as I could.

During that first year or so after my move to Nashville, I met a lot of people that God would use to demonstrate certain things to me. One of them was a lady named Jasmine, who became a friend for a season and someone from whom I learned a lot. One of the things I took away from my friendship with

Jasmine was knowing how and when to pray over one's house. I visited her at her house quite a bit.

One time I remember was when a male neighbor of hers came to her house just being friendly, to talk. He had been drinking, so he was acting a little off. Once the man left, Jasmine asked me to follow her around and pray for her as she prayed over the house because she sensed something different about the man. I did just that. We placed our hands on the walls and walked around asking God to remove any and everything that was in there that didn't belong.

Jasmine was a huge advocate for protecting her peace, and I saw how important that was. That's one thing I took away from that relationship. Soon, I started praying over my mother and sisters when they were asleep. There would be times when God would just lead me in the middle of the night to walk through my mother's house laying my hands on the doors, windows, couches, my sisters' heads, and my mother's door, praying over everything. I could never lay my hands on my mother's head, though, because she was such a light sleeper; she probably would have woken up.

That was a great and vital part of faith that I learned and still use today in my own home. All this time, Eric and I had kept in touch. He came to visit me once a month over a six-month period. He seemed to be a changed person, but I really didn't know.

After about seven months, I convinced my mother to let Eric move to Tennessee and in with us. Wrong move!! If you are a parent and you're reading this, please, and I repeat, *Please never let your kid's boyfriend/girlfriend come live with you!* The mother of one of my female cousins once allowed my cousin's boyfriend to move in with them when she was only sixteen. I remember thinking, "She's crazy for allowing that." I was fifteen at the time when I witnessed that, and I remember thinking how my mom would never allow that. It's funny how that turned out for me, arranging it so that my boyfriend could move in with us. It's the very same situation that, several years earlier, I had never seen myself getting into.

Under conditions put down by my mom, Eric had to help pay the bills and eventually be out of the house by a certain time, and, of course, we could not sleep in the same bed. The deadline for him to move out to his own place was three months, but that turned into six.

Looking back, I believe my mom allowed him to move in with us because she wanted me to stay in Tennessee and not move back to Ohio. She herself had moved to Nashville alone, without family or a lot of friends—just my sisters and me. She probably would have done anything to keep me in Nashville. Sometimes I wish she would have just been honest with me and told me exactly how she felt at the time; that way, I could have made the best decision, or at least considered it.

After Eric moved to Nashville, things started out OK, but soon I found evidence on his phone that he had been entertaining other females he knew back in Ohio. We were still fighting and arguing as well, but it was like this had become the norm for me. I had become numb to it. I didn't know what caused me to hold onto things that I should have let go of long before. Possibly it was a lack of self-love, if I knew who I was— and whose I was—at the time, I wouldn't have tolerated it.

Eventually, my mom got fed up with my being there and his starting to disrespect me in her presence. Such as throwing a drink in my face while we were all in the car going somewhere. Then there was the arguing between Eric and me, as well as my doing whatever I wanted to do, like sneaking downstairs at night to lie with Eric. Mom had had enough of this nonsense and eventually told both of us we needed to move out and find a place of our own. It was one big mess.

Eric and I had good days, and we had our bad days. Not to anyone's surprise, I thought the good outweighed the bad, but whenever someone is putting their hands on you, that takes the cake, *period*, in my mind! Eric had gotten better after a while. We weren't arguing as much by the time we got ready to move back, nor were we fighting. Still, we had to come up with a plan to move back to Ohio, two to three months at the most, and then move to North Carolina to be with his mother. The plan was that once we got to North Carolina, we would stay with his mother for a while, get jobs, and stack money until we got our own place. It sounded so perfect, like a great idea.

I was for the plan, so I left my mother and sisters once again for the second time and returned to Dayton with Eric. Once I got there, I went and stayed with my cousin—we're just a little over a year apart in age. I really didn't want to go back to Dayton because I was over it, but I went along with it, because I knew Dayton was just a stopover on our way to North Carolina. Of course, I kept in touch with Eric and his mom for the next three months in Dayton, just trying to figure out the details on what was going on and when she would be ready for us in North Carolina.

As each month went by, the move date was getting pushed back further and further. It went from us moving in May, to July, then to August. I didn't know what the holdup was, but I soon realized that God was holding up that move for a reason. Eric and I were in the truck one day, heading to the mall. I was driving, and at one point I sparked up a conversation concerning church. Eric's aunt had invited us to her church, and I told him I wanted *us* to go that Sunday. I was always trying to involve him in things that God told me to do. Just like when I was nineteen and God spoke to me, telling me to stop having sex! Period. He told me to remain abstinent.

"I think you should become celibate with me," I said to Eric as we drove. I wasn't mature enough at the time to say, "Hey, look this is what God has told me to do. If you're with it, let's go; if not, I'll have to holler!" When I mentioned the celibate thing, he told me straight up, "I don't think that's going to work." In my little perfect world, however, it could work—I believed that. I told him that if we just tried hard enough to resist and prayed when we got tempted, we would be OK. He still wasn't going for it.

So, he got mad and said he didn't want to go to the church due to him saying the service would be too long! One thing led to another, and what was once a conversation had now turned into a heated discussion. I yelled out, "*You are acting like a bi---!!*" but before I could get the whole word out, Eric's fist hit full force on the right side of my jaw. This hit was unlike any other I had ever gotten from him. It was like all my senses had just been knocked into me (at least when it came to him).

I yelled out, "You are acting like a bi---!!" but before I could get the whole word out, Eric's fist hit full force on the right side of my jaw. This hit was unlike any other I had ever gotten from him.

I didn't fight him back like I normally would have. I didn't yell, and I didn't curse. I just looked over at him and quickly turned back to focus on the road. I made a detour and instead of continuing to the mall, I headed to his place to drop him off there. I pulled up at the house, but he wouldn't get out of the truck. I repeatedly told him it was over and to get out, but he wasn't leaving. So, I got out of the truck, ran up to the front door of the house, and beat on the door as loudly, urgently, and thunderously as I could, but no one came to the door.

Eric then came up behind me, and in a bold manner told me, "I don't know why you're knocking on the door. I can let you in!" As he was taking the key out of his pocket to open the door, I ran back to the truck, jumped in, and locked the doors. I looked down to fasten my seat belt, and when I looked back up, he was already on the passenger side, beating on the window and yelling, "*Open the damn door!*"

Having already started the truck, I looked down to put the truck into reverse and backed up at a high rate of speed. Everything was happening within a blink of an eye. As I'm backing up, I see Eric out of my peripheral vision fall as if something had pulled him down with a strong force. I immediately stopped the truck, but when I did I heard him beating on the car, screaming, "Bitch, get off my leg!!! You are on me, stupid bitch, get the fuck off my leg!"

I quickly put the truck back into drive and went forward, also noticing his grandmother standing in the door. I got out of the truck and she asked me, "What is going on out here?"

"Granny, he has put his hands on me for the last time. I'm done; I can't do it."

By this time, Eric had gotten up and his leg—the one that was run over—was bleeding. He could barely walk, and he asked me to take him to the hospital. I wasn't *that* heartless, and I hadn't intended to run over him in the first place. I took him to the hospital and dropped him off there, and as I did I knew this time I was done with him.

It wasn't an hour later that he called me asking me to come join him at the hospital. He left voice messages and text messages, but I never responded to any of it.

That evening, I called my mother to tell her what had happened, and again she was there for me. She told me she would come to Dayton the following weekend to get me. Although my mother and I had a rough relationship and never understood one another, she was there in cases like this when I needed her the most! The next day, as planned, I went to the church service with Eric's aunt and mom. They weren't too delighted with what had transpired between Eric and me the day before.

When we got to the service and listened to the pastor preaching, I heard confirmation! I remember his saying, "You have all this mess going on in your relationship; you're fighting and arguing, and there is no glory in that!" I knew this was the work of the Holy Spirit because a similar message—*very* similar message—had been preached by my bishop back at my home church in Nashville. The pastor continued with his message, and it was so powerful that I couldn't stop the tears from falling.

Toward the end of the service, the preacher announced an altar call, and his words were, "There are seven people in here where God has been talking to you, but you haven't been listening. I need you to come to the altar immediately." As soon as he said that, I knew I needed to get up and go down there, but I felt scared. I was a visitor at this church, where no one knew me; I was nervous. I sat there in the back of the church with tears rolling down my face, hurt and knowing I needed to go, but I sat there. The pastor then said, "Young lady sitting in the far back with the brown sweater on, come here." That lady was me!

My heart dropped. I was shocked, like why did this man just call me out? I went to the altar with tears rolling down my face. I tried to suppress them, but they kept pouring down. Suddenly, the pastor and I were face to face. He then said, "God says, 'Let it go.' You have so much love inside of you, but God wants you to use it for the kingdom *first*." He went on to say some other things, and I just stood there in disbelief, because I knew this moment was divine order.

It all had come to me in that moment. The fight that Eric and I had the day before hurt, but it was needed. God needed me to be at the service alone so that I could receive what he needed me to receive with no distractions. I understood it in that moment. I left the church with that understanding. I also knew that Eric and I would never again be together, and we haven't been.

I still had to stay in Dayton for another week. That Wednesday, Eric showed up at my aunt's house, where I had been staying, with a ring asking me to marry him. He apologized, as always, and pulled out the ring from his pocket and asked if we could start over. I looked at the ring as he held it. Many thoughts went through my mind at the time, but they didn't last long. He said, "You're not even going to take the ring out of the box? Put it on!" Something came over me and I blurted out, "*No!* I can't do it." He looked at me as if he couldn't believe I said no, but I did and I stood firm on that. I then told him he had to go. He left, and that was the last time I saw Eric for a long time.

A Letter to Shay

Dear Shay,

Pretty girl, pretty girl, pretty girl, you are supposed to be here! Yes, you've encountered some things, but don't lose hope. Sure, you haven't had an easy start, and you feel as if the world is against you, but I promise if you just hold on, things will begin to turn around. In all things, take your time. Don't rush anything. Everything that you need or want will come to you when it is supposed to. One of the reasons you haven't received things that you want is because you just are not mentally or emotionally ready to receive them.

Know that you are exactly where you are meant to be; yes, even with all the craziness that has gone on. Soon there will be purpose in all your pain. Love hard, but love *yourself first*! You cannot make a man who is not ready for a relationship be with you! You can't force anything on anyone! If that person really wanted you, you would know and be able to tell it through all their actions!

Never compromise anything, for anyone. Especially 1) if you don't see the relationship going anywhere, and 2) if your love, time, and heartfelt sentiments are not being reciprocated. Don't worry about "friends." A lot of the people you meet on this journey will only serve you for a season.

Get what you need to get, be the same you, and move on! Never allow anyone to change you. *Stay the same sweet person* no matter how many times you're afflicted by others. Know what not to put up with, but don't become the same type of person that has wronged you.

You have been blessed and I need you to know the difference between lifetime, seasonal, and reason relationships—male or female. Remember to "measure twice, cut once." You are the prize and you are the catch!! Know that! *Love* is not merely a word, but a *fruit*! And if you pay attention long enough, people will reveal themselves—listen twice as much as you speak!

Stop giving your all to everyone! This includes people who come into your life and claim to be friends, or even guys who come around and show the slightest interest. It is OK to date! Hear me when I say "date" and not sleep around, because not everyone needs or deserves your body. You don't need a thug or someone who you feel can "handle you." You need someone who is strong and courageous! Someone who loves God just as much as you and someone who loves you more than or as much as *you* love you! That's the key; you have to love you, and you have to think, and not only think but want differently for yourself. It's really a heart and mind matter!

Everything will be OK. You still have lots of learning to do and none of the things that I told will come to you overnight. But once you've matured more, and learn who rules your life, things will start to move smoothly. I can see you in the future, and it looks *sooooo* bright!!! I love you!

Until next time,
Da'Shay

6

Do You Really Want to be Free?

Jeremiah 2:19-20
"Your wickedness will punish you; your backsliding will rebuke you. Consider then and realize how evil and bitter it is for you when you forsake the Lord your God and have no awe of me, declares the Lord, the Lord Almighty. 'Long ago you broke off your yoke and tore off your bonds'; you said, 'I will not transgress!' But, on every high hill and under every green tree, you lay down playing the harlot!'"

"Wouldn't it be great to enter into a relationship without being so thirsty for love that you can't trust your own discernment? When you are not thirsty for love, you can make better decisions."
— T. D. JAKES

SOME WOMEN LIKE ME GO THROUGH THINGS OVER AND OVER and over, and we still just don't get it. Although I was going to church and had somewhat of a growing relationship with Jesus, I still was doing what I wanted to do. I was hopping from

81

one situation to the next with no regret. In one instance, I began talking to a guy that I met at a party through mutual friends. His name was Andre.

Over the course of the next year, Andre had become the "broken love" (the kind of love where you'd experience great pain, deceit, and lies). Looking back, I can see how I went from one relationship to the next, which is what tends to happen in most cases with broken females. We don't take that time to heal. We hop from this one to that one, and we end up in the same cycle with the same "type of guy," just wrapped in a different package.

Andre was indeed different from Eric and other guys to whom I was typically attracted. Over the first few months of our dating, I compared Andre to Eric a lot. Andre was educated; he had his own place, he played golf, and he came from a good background. He was sweet, and he wasn't hood. I found all these reasons as to why he was better than the last one and perfect for me. This situation started off wrong; all I saw from him was the physical. I didn't mind it at the time. I was using it as a healing mechanism, although in the moment I didn't realize that was what I was doing.

I didn't care about what I was doing, though, because I would think about Eric cheating and how he treated me. I got to a point where I was using this situation along with others as a means to get past the past, when in fact all I was doing was causing more damage to my soul and heart.

Andre was in college at Tennessee State University, and he was from Dayton. While I was there waiting on my mom to come pick me up and take me back to Nashville, he just so happened to be in town, so we spent the last few days of my being there together. Once I got back to Nashville, in December 2012, I returned to my home church, moved back in with my mom, and jumped right into what turned into a three-year, off-and-on situation with Andre.

The crazy thing about this situation was I had all the clues of this not being the right thing for me, yet I was determined that I would keep riding this one in hopes that one day Andre would pull it all together. After all, I had thought I had found something better. Which he was, but he just wasn't better for me.

Over the next three weeks after my return to Nashville, Andre and I began to spend a lot of time together. I went over to his house, if not every day at least every other day. I didn't have a closely wrapped, tight relationship with God at the time, but I did know how to do one thing and that was *pray!* I had really started to vibe with Andre. I knew quickly that I liked him, a lot, so I needed to know if I should be dealing with him or not. I learned so much from this situation, but one thing stands out: *Do not pray for God to reveal or show you anything unless you are truly ready to see what you've asked him to show you!* God chases the ones he loves, and he will see to it that you aren't out there looking dumb. If you are, it's clearly your own fault. As I mentioned before, we all have warning signs, and if you really are paying attention they'll be vivid.

I began to pray and ask God to reveal Andre to me. I liked him, but I needed his heart to be revealed. It didn't take long for me to get an answer. The following week, after I had prayed, I was over at Andre's house hanging out with him and a few of his friends. Suddenly, there was a loud knocking at the door, over and over. At first, I thought it might have been the police because of the way it sounded. A friend of his went to the door and told everyone to be quiet. He played it as if whoever was at the door was someone for him. Being the naïve female that I was at the time, I believed it . . . until I heard the girl yell out *"If you don't open this door, I'm going to mess up your truck!"* I looked around the room knowing that no one in the room had a truck, except for Andre! I then realized this angry female banging on the door was there for Andre.

When we had first started dating, he had told me he wasn't dating anyone and that he was solely interested in me. Back in the present: I was confused, forgetting that this is what I had prayed about and that this was a sign—an answer from God. Andre never opened the door for this girl, but he talked to her through the door, threatening to call the police, and she eventually left.

I figured once she left, he would explain to me in detail what had just happened, but he didn't. All he told me was that she didn't matter, that she had been calling all day and just decided to show up! I let it roll off my back, and I stayed the night. After getting out of the shower the next day, I was drying myself off, bending over to get to my legs and feet, when I notice lots of hair on the floor. It was female hair; lots of it. That was my second sign, although I continued to ignore them.

I asked Andre about the hair on the floor. He told me that the hair was old—that it had been there a long time—that it came from a female he used to talk to in the summertime. *Lies*! He kept feeding me lies because I allowed him to. That was my biggest mistake, putting all my eggs in one basket and not listening to all the warnings I had. Just silly of me, but the whole situation was also a great lesson for me. I now know that God will let us continue to hit the same brick wall until we decide that this isn't what we want or need.

Andre seemed so innocent when I met him. I put him on a pedestal. I said to myself, "Well, he's not a thug, so he won't dog me like the thug I've had in the past." I thought Andre was different, more mature, more of a caring, responsible person. It's humorous to me now, but to me at the time, I truly judged him off his status. He was in school, played golf, and came from a two-parent home (those were my thoughts)! I was sadly mistaken; unfortunately, I was about to embark on a three-year journey of self-inflicted pain with this person.

Time went on, and it was like each month brought a new revelation as to what Andre had been doing behind my back. Honestly, it became plain. It went from one thing to another. He was sloppy, and I was an investigator. I saw more hair on the floor. I saw Valentine's Day cards, lip gloss, a head scarf behind the bed, and much more. I didn't know what it was going to take for me to leave this man; clearly, he didn't respect me enough to stop messing with me and another female at the same time. I even had a dream to show me what was going on, but I still didn't fully comprehend it until I was out of the situation.

One night while asleep, I had a dream that I went over to Andre's house while he and I weren't speaking to one another. In the dream I initiated the conversation, just like I always did in real life! I showed up at his house in the dream, and the other young woman he had been dealing with opened the door. I asked her where Andre was, and she replied, "In the room." I headed back to the bedroom and she followed me. I entered the bedroom, and there Andre was. He got into the bed, and I followed behind him, lying down right down next to him, and the other woman he had been dealing with got right in the bed with us, and I woke up from the dream right after that.

This dream had me going crazy for a while, but I immediately realized what it was that God was saying to me. God was telling me there was another woman involved, regardless of if she was the main chick or the chick on the side; either way, she's involved and he's sleeping with *both* of us! I had that information but still just didn't get it.

I was growing tired of all the nonsense with Andre and me, but I remained with him. I should have gotten the clue, right? I never met his parents, never went out on any real dates with him. We "dated" for the longest time, however with no real destination or direction. It was as if he was keeping me under wraps.

All the things that had transpired between the two of us happened rather quickly. The things that were being revealed to me were revealed within a six-month span, but the back and forth continued for three whole years. In my mind, we were going to make this work. It didn't make things any better when I would find out more things about him and attempt to muster up the strength to leave; he would say things like "Don't leave me. We will make this work. Just please ... don't leave me."

This situation was all manipulation. Andre apparently knew what to say to me to get me to stay. My mind was so jacked up, I just didn't care. Every time I would find out something new, I would pray and ask God to help me get out of the situation, but then I would turn right back around and go back to the very thing that contributed to my broken mess I had going on inside. Proverbs 26:11 states, "As a dog returns to his vomit, so does a fool return to his folly." I was that fool. I was hooked. Every time I would try to leave, or at least want to leave, something would pull me back. I believed this was a negative soul tie.

Andre and I lived about thirty miles apart. My place of employment was right up the street from my apartment. When Andre would call me, I would pick regardless of the time, no matter if it was midnight or 2 A.M. If he asked me to come over, I would get up, grab my things, and go right over. It didn't matter that I had to be at work at 7 a.m. It didn't matter that I was tired, I was so gone in the head; I did anything he asked. Do you think I got any reciprocation from him, something to show me he genuinely cared about me? No . . . not one time. Yet I remained there, in what my pastor stated was a mental cave!

Do you think I left? *No!* I stayed, but toward what would be the end, I knew what I needed to do. You see, I was already broken mentally and emotionally. In 2 Corinthians 10:4-6, my favorite scripture, it states that we must use spiritual weapons to war against things of the spirit.

This was a battle unlike any I had ever dealt with. This battle was spiritual. There was a stronghold on me, and for some reason I could not break free. I kept holding on. Part of the reason initially was because I didn't want to be free. I had self-sabotaged myself.

This was a battle unlike any I had ever dealt with. This battle was spiritual. There was a stronghold on me, and for some reason I could not break free. I kept holding on. Part of the reason initially was because I didn't want to be free. I had self-sabotaged myself, which we sometimes do as I mentioned in chapter 3, "Dysfunctionally Functional," by listening to or watching others. By doing that, our whole perception gets tainted when it comes to men because of what we grew up around or what we were accustomed to.

We take anything because we don't know who we are, or we aren't taught how a man/woman is supposed to treat us. I was emotionally broken like other women out there, and I was carrying over anger from my childhood, things that happened to me. I resented my mother for a long time. Some women are depressed. I dealt with that in my younger years, carrying hatred, loneliness, abandonment, feelings of emptiness, disbelief, low self-esteem, grief. What we must do to get free is bring all these feelings and combat them with the word of God.

"Casting down imaginations, and every high thing that exalts itself against the knowledge of God, and bringing every thought into captivity to the obedience of Christ and being ready to punish all disobedience when your obedience is fulfilled." (2 Corinthians 10:5-6)

As much as we might have had unwanted generational curses passed down, things spoken over our lives, family and friends sabotaging us, once we come into full knowledge of who God is and what he has done for us and, lastly, what his word says about us, there is no excuse as to why we aren't *free*! At that point, you just don't want to be free. The real test comes when you can take those thoughts that come into your head to discourage you and cast them back to where they came from (being ready to punish all disobedience). I learned this the hard way.

For years I was rebuking the air, trying to punish something that I clearly had no control over because my obedience was unfulfilled. You cannot and, I repeat, you cannot fully move past something or someone that you continually allow to come back into your life. It will come back stronger and harder every trip. T. D. Jakes said in one of his sermons that I tuned into, "You can't cast down something you just got out of the bed with."

This hit home for me! The scripture that was in the beginning of the chapter from Jeremiah, where God was saying, "Hey, you've asked me to continually save you, I have repeatedly; and you said you wouldn't go back, but every chance you get, you lay down playing the prostitute!" That scripture was actually sent to me "accidentally" in our natural realm, but I know God needed me to see that. My spiritual mother (Michelle) meant to send me a different scripture; same chapter just different verse.

When I read the Bible verse you see at the beginning of this chapter, my eyes filled with tears because I knew I needed to do what God had asked me to do years prior to this moment, and that was to remain *celibate*. God needed me all to himself. I couldn't possibly cast out the lustful thoughts that continually entered my mind because I hadn't been fully obedient to God's word. Furthermore, I couldn't possibly be freed from these dysfunctional situations if I wasn't being obedient. When you become obedient, your vision becomes clear.

If God keeps telling me to stop engaging in a certain thing, let's say sex . . . and I continue with it, because it feels good, I'm left with the emotional weight of it all. Then I'm crying to God, like "Lord, save me," but he's like, "I told you not to get involved in that manner to begin with, especially with that person."

Part of the reason a lot of us struggle with emotional torment is because we don't obey what God told us long ago to do.

- We must fulfill our obedience in order to be able to punish all disobedience.
- To women with children and/or a husband: Until you obey your husband and God, your kids will continue to disobey, and you wonder why. It's probably because you aren't in order.

I have put together a few prerequisites to a healthy self-esteem:

- Recognize the need for God.
- Evaluate your commitment to God.
- Go when God tells you to go! Your disobedience could affect the plans of God.
- Have a realistic view of yourself.
- Avoid comparisons of yourself with others.
- Rest in ownership by God (know that he knows best).

7
Don't Take the Bait

Matthew 10:16
"Behold, I am sending you out like sheep among wolves.
Therefore, be as wise as snakes and as innocent as doves."

2 Timothy 3:5-7
"Having a form of godliness but denying its power. Have
nothing to do with such people. They are the kind who
worm their way into homes and gain control over gullible
women who are loaded down with sins and are swayed
by all kinds of evil desires, always learning but never
able to come to a knowledge of the truth."

OFTENTIMES THROUGHOUT OUR LIVES, WE COME TO A POINT where we must take either the high road or the lower. We have these tough decision-making moments in which we must figure out if we will follow the desire to do what is right, or will we take the easy route and do wrong. No matter how badly you've been hurt, be it in a previous relationship, feeling neglected by a parent, or hurt by church people (which, I might add, is the *worse* hurt, in my opinion, one could ever encounter), or no matter how much you've been influenced by family and close friends, you must *never* allow that hurt to take up residency in your heart or mind to where you allow that one emotion to control the decisions you make.

A lesson I learned throughout this season of rational decision-making is that hurt people hurt people, even if it's unintentional! A lot of people don't even know they're hurting. Some people hurt from marital situations, some people hurt from past relationships, some people hurt for money, a lot of us hurt for love; whatever it is you're hurting from, you must first identify the issue, confront it, and then take the necessary steps to heal yourself. It's extremely important to resist the urge to do what your flesh wants to do.

During this time of my life, I felt as if I had no one to talk to. No one! My father was there for me during this season, but he's so real, raw, and uncut sometimes. I needed someone to pray with me and just be there.

Sometimes doing the right thing is extremely difficult! Sometimes we even *want* to do wrong. I know I've had a few of those moments. But you cannot give up nor give in, because the testing is only for a season. Typically, your biggest test comes right before your biggest blessing.

I remember a time where I was put to the test! It was one crazy situation after the next. It was like: OK, she passed this test; let's hit her with another, and another, and another." During this time of my life, I felt as if I had no one to talk to. *No one!* My father was there for me during this season, but he's so real, raw, and uncut sometimes. I needed someone to pray with me and just be there. Granted, I had my godmother Michelle there and her husband Doug, but I think my main thing was wanting a person physically there at all times to guide me, tell me my next steps, and tell me what's ahead, and I just didn't have that. I felt alone.

It was time to find out, was I really about that faith life? Was I really a woman of God? I had to not only talk about it, but I had to walk it out and be about it. I had literally been sent out as a sheep among wolves. One of the first tests concerned a friend I had met when I moved to Nashville. It was one of the first females here who I considered an actual friend.

Her name was Vivian. I met Vivian in 2013, and we just clicked. I began to go over to her house and hang out with her and her family. I admired Vivian. Where I come from, there weren't too many humble females with whom I happened to have an encounter. She was extremely humble and sweet, with a spirit as bright as gold! Vivian was already a very beautiful woman, but her spirit and humility made her shine so much brighter. I am a *firm* believer that God sends people in our lives to demonstrate certain things to us: love, kindness, meekness, you name it, especially if you're lacking it.

God uses his people as instruments, and I've had the pleasure of meeting a few of his people through which he used to teach me great things. Vivian, in particular, taught me many things. To start with, like I said earlier, she was such a humble person. At the point in my life when I met Vivian, I was extremely materialistic. I thought I couldn't shop anywhere but the mall; everything needed to be a name brand—nothing could be from a thrift store! That in itself was one of the major ways in which God helped me to see *me!* I started to notice from being around Vivian how happy she was, and how content she was with just the small things: a pair of used shoes, a used coat . . . I mean anything.

God's light radiated through this woman. I was led to pray for myself through watching her, and I experienced deliverance concerning being materialistic. The light that was inside of her exposed my darkness in that area of knowing I had that issue of being extremely materialistic inside me. I hung tight with Vivian for a while, and her family taught me some very valuable things as well.

She had a nice family. Like all families, I'm sure they had their issues, but they weren't exposed in public, certainly not around me. Her parents where still married and had been married for more than twenty years. Her father was a great big, caring man, extremely loving to his wife, and the wife was nice, classy, and elegant. She had two brothers and grandparents who had been married for a long time as well.

Being around this family made me yearn for such a relationship with my own immediate family. Since I had come from a place of brokenness, I never truly was able to experience this with my mother, father, sisters, and cousins. By being around this, I knew God was showing me something. I saw how a father loves his baby girl and cares for her *consistently*. I saw how a mother not only allows her daughter to confide in her, but she also comes right back and gives the same thing with no judgment or shame. I saw what I'd never seen before, something which I'd always wanted. Although I know that it wasn't perfect—nothing is, everything just seemed so perfect with Vivian's family. No way, shape, or form was I jealous that I hadn't experienced it; I was just happy to see black love.

Since I was a "new Christian," I had a pair of cute rose gold-colored glasses, figuratively speaking, that I purchased upon my arrival to Nashville. I believed that everyone in church could do *no* wrong. I was so naïve. I thought that everyone had a great big heart and wouldn't do anything to hurt or harm me, or themselves for that matter. I was sadly mistaken and found that out on a Saturday night, when Vivian and I were set to hang out.

I was on my way over to Vivian's apartment, assuming we were just going to hang out, but when I got there, she was on the phone. After about five minutes of this, she turned and asked me, "You wanna go to Memphis tonight?"

"Sure," I said, without even knowing who's there, why we were going, or how we were getting there.

She asked me if I wanted to ride there, and I said yes, no question. She told her friend, a male, on the phone that we'd be leaving in thirty minutes, and she would call him again once we got to town.

We got on the road and drove for three hours, westward toward Memphis. Once we arrived in Memphis, we pulled up to an extremely nice house. A tall, bald, brown-skinned guy—attractive I might add—walked out to the garage to greet Vivian and me. We got out of our car and into his truck, and we went on a midnight tour of Memphis.

After the tour, we pulled up to a salsa club. I had never been salsa dancing. I wasn't opposed to it; "Why not give it a try?" I thought to myself. We went in and danced for a while. Vivian's friend danced with us as well; it was a great night. We stayed at the salsa club all night until it was time to close, and by then I was *beat*! When we arrived back to his house, I was again amazed at how beautiful it was.

Once inside, we walked past a great big piano and headed upstairs to the guest room, where Vivian and I were to stay. He offered us towels to take a shower and food and water. Upon entering the room. I saw pictures all over. I remember being so sleepy and just lying right down. Vivian, staring at the pictures, picks one up. "*Gosh*! She is so beautiful!" I heard her say, "She looks just like me."

"Who are you talking about?!" I asked.

"*His wife!*"

I instantly got up.

"His wife!" I was in total shock!

"Well, they're separated. She lives all the way in another state, and he's here."

While looking at all the pictures of his wife, I couldn't believe my twenty-one-year-old self was standing in the home of married man who was sleeping with my friend. His wife definitely had a lot in common with Vivian—bone structure in the face, same hairstyle, same body shape. I mean, it was spooky!

I really had nothing much to say on the topic of her seeing this man. I was young and not too mature in the manner that would even speak out against someone else's faults. I felt I had too many of my own. All I knew was that I saw that growing up. I never wanted to be a part of it. I always said I would never mess with a married man. I always felt bad for the wife.

I didn't cast any judgments against Vivian. I just said to myself, "OK" and went on about getting myself to sleep. We got up early the next day and headed back to Nashville to change and get to church.

I know it's not right, but at the time I just couldn't help but look at Vivian differently. A part of that was my fault for having her up on a pedestal. I saw her to be a positive role model, a big sister who could do no wrong, and what she was doing didn't make her any less than any of that. But learned that just because people are in church and "seem" a certain way doesn't make things that way. We are *all* the same. *Everyone* has a struggle.

I just wasn't mature enough at the time to realize people in church make mistakes, too. Church is merely a hospital with a lot of sick people, spiritually speaking. Perhaps Vivian messed up her Christian witness, at least in my eyes, but I learned a valuable lesson. Some time had passed, and I found out a year and a half into my friendship that Vivian had gotten into a relationship with a man named George.

George was cool, and it seemed he had kept Vivian happy from what I had seen in the beginning. Since I was one of the girlfriends always around her and I was single, a typical guy move was to try and hook me up with their buddy or say they had a friend who wanted to talk to me. At least, that's something I always went through .

One day when Viv and I were together, she and George were on a video chat, when George told her to tell me his younger brother Antonio wanted to talk to me. I was skeptical of it because I didn't know him, and second, I had never done any hookups, not since I was sixteen, and we all know how that went. I immediately said no. Although Vivian tried hard to convince me, I wasn't going. She asked me at least three times before she finally got the clue that I just wasn't going to go on a date with him. Plus, at the time, I was still off and on with my own "situationships."

I had very few encounters with George in the beginning because he lived out of town, but he and Vivian skyped all the time—at least that's what I saw when she and I were together. Later that year, Vivian and her family were planning a family vacation and had invited me to go with them, and I accepted. We went to Savannah, Georgia. I absolutely loved this place! It was my first time visiting the city, and I fell in love. That's when I had met Vivian's boyfriend for the first time. I didn't know he would be there, but he popped up and surprised her; her parents were in on the surprise which was sweet.

A day into our being in Savannah, we were heading to view the city when I received text messages from an unknown number. Upon opening the messages, I saw pictures of George standing next to his artwork (George was a painter). I was sort of confused as to why he was sending me those pictures.

With Vivian in the back seat next to me, I asked her, "Did you give George my number? I just got some pictures from him."

"Yes. He asked for it in the hotel room."

Her father then asked, "Viv, why didn't he send *you* the picture?"

She said it was because her phone wasn't receiving them at the moment. Like with her dad, it seemed fishy to me as well, but I didn't say anything. I just went on and enjoyed the rest of our vacation.

About three weeks after we returned to Nashville, Vivian notified me that some of George's work would be in an art exhibit and asked if I wanted to go with her to the viewing. "Sure," I said. I was her friend and I had nothing else to do that night, so why not?

I got to the exhibit and the work was amazing. After Vivian, her father, mother, and I had viewed all the work, we later took pictures with George and his brothers. At the time, I was single, so, technically of course, I was scoping out the brothers—but just looking. Upon us walking up to meet George and his family, I looked at all of them, and there was only one that I found attractive, who, I found out later, was the oldest brother. As I'm scoping him out from head to toe, as women do, I saw a wedding ring on his finger, and the radar went off.

We finished taking pictures, and I was then introduced to everyone. I also finally saw the younger brother, Antonio, who they were trying to get me to date. It was a great evening. Once the event was over, we all left, and I returned home. A week or two passed and I hadn't really talked much to Vivian in that time because I had been busy and I knew she had as well. On a Friday night, I received a text from George asking me what was I doing. I texted back to him I was watching a movie with one of my friends. He went on to tell me that he was in the car with Vivian heading to her parents' house for dinner and someone had wanted to take me to dinner.

Because they all were from out of town, they were staying at a hotel, the Gaylord. He told me to go and meet the older married brother at the hotel. That right there rubbed me the wrong way for multiple reasons. I was thinking he was talking about the younger brother, who they had been trying to get me to talk to. He corrected me and notified me that he was talking about the oldest brother! He said, "He was drooling when he saw you!!" My response was, "*He's married!*" George texted back and said, "He's separated!!"

I didn't care if you were separated or together, it's all the same thing if you are married. Plus, he was still wearing his ring; he's married, *period*. At once I was offended and told George I wasn't going. I felt as if he was treating me like a call girl! Like, "Oh, he's at the hotel. Go out there to see him!!" Keep in mind I was twenty-one. The man who supposedly only wanted to take me to dinner was forty-three! George said, "Well, he's not trying to marry you. He just wants to talk to you, and take you to dinner!"

I knew what he wanted, but I wasn't going! Once George sensed through my texts how livid I was, he apologized and told me multiple times how beautiful I was and how I should be showered with love, gifts, etc. I knew that I was beautiful, but I wasn't about to fall into his trap, either. I said thanks, but I was still angry.

I couldn't wait to talk to Vivian. The next day I had that text exchange with George on my mind the whole day at work. I hadn't talked to Viv yet, but I called her as soon as I got off work. She said how she'd been thinking about me. I was steaming!!

"Viv!!, why did you allow him to try to hook me up with his *married brother*!? You know what I've been through. You know I don't play that."

I instantly came off with an attitude. She said she didn't know anything about George trying to set me up with the married brother. In fact, when they were in the car, Vivian said that George asked her, "Is Da'Shay's number still the same? Someone wants to take her to dinner." She said she told him that it was. She also said that she said to George, "Oh, OK, Antonio. I see you!" She thought he was speaking of the younger brother, and George just smiled.

Snake! Why wouldn't he tell her he was speaking of the older, married brother? She asked me what George and I talked about while we texted. I told her everything—every single detail. I even screenshot all the messages and sent them to her just to be clear on my end.

When she saw how many times he had called me "beautiful" and said little things to me, she asked if that made me uncomfortable. I was totally honest with her; I told her it did. I wasn't just going to come out and say how uncomfortable I was, because I know how some females can react when it comes to their men with whom they're in a relationship. I felt, if you ever must question that—that is, question what he said and if it made you uncomfortable—nine times out of ten, the person for whom you have those questions is in the wrong.

I felt a release once I got off the phone with her. I felt a little better also knowing that I had gotten off my chest what I needed to, knowing that she had nothing to do with his trying to set me up with his married brother.

The next day I received a five-page apology from George. Something he wrote stuck with me from that message he sent; it's the part where he stated the reason he wanted me to go to the hotel/dinner with his brother was that his brother had been going through some problems at home, and he wanted to help him get his mind off all the *pain* that he was experiencing! That alone made me block out everything else he said because I knew it was bogus.

Other than providing something sexual for him, what could I have possibly done to take his mind off the pain? What could we possibly talk about? I was twenty-one. Men like that, who are hurting, will treat you like a piece of meat if you let them. They will use you for what they want, then go back home to their wives, leaving you all alone, battling spirits that have attached themselves to you through that person.

I might have made some silly mistakes, but I wasn't about to make one in that situation! I knew better. After that, the very thing I sort of feared would happen, did happen. Vivian became distant with me. I'm not sure what I had done. She claimed it was due to her being extremely busy at school, but I knew that wasn't the case and what the reason was.

It truly hurt me at first because I had considered her to be a close friend—more than a friend, in fact; she was family, at least I thought she was. I reached out when I first noticed she was drifting away. Sometimes I wouldn't get a response. Going months without seeing each other and weeks without talking was a drastic change.

Back then I was desperate for friendship. I was in Nashville alone, and this was still a new place for me; I didn't know anyone here. All my friends lived far away, and upon my moving to Nashville, I had had to let go of a lot of them just because of God having us on different pages. I soon had to realize this was what God was doing with me and Vivian. I had to realize that she was in my life to serve a purpose for just a season. I had to let go.

I had to be OK with the lesson, and I had to move on accordingly, no matter if I felt heavily invested into this friendship or not. I had to be OK with the removal of people. I had to be OK with my dry season of being alone. In that aloneness, I found out who God was, and there again he was building me up to get ready to continue going through challenges.

8
Broken, but Healed

Matthew 7:6
"Do not give what is holy to the dogs, and do not cast your pearls before swine, Lest they trample them under their feet, and they turn and tear you into pieces."

A S I AM WRITING THIS LAST (FULL) CHAPTER, I CAN'T HELP BUT be puzzled and raise this question to myself: Why on earth did it take me this long to be obedient!? Why didn't I get it five years ago? Why did I have to go through the pain, and then put myself through self-inflicted pain? Why didn't I get it after the first heartbreak?

While all the questions are very important, and I do want answers, I must accept that some things are just not preventable. I also must know, just as you must know, that when it comes to pain that we bring upon ourselves, we will continue to go through the pain until we grow through the lesson. In fact, if you fail, it will be the exact same test, just packaged a different way.

I have a great relationship with God; that's probably why he's kept me for this long, so why didn't I listen? To be frank, in most cases, I just wasn't ready. Sometimes I didn't even pray to him about a particular issue because I already knew that I wasn't supposed to be doing it.

In this part of my life, I had seen so many things in church and with different people, I had gotten to a point where I said to myself, "Well . . . the people in church are the same as the ones out in the world, so I might as well deal with the same ones whom I was dealing with in the first place.

I had fled from the presence of God. I found myself going backward in yet another pointless/purposeless situationship. I had begun dating a guy that I had known since I was a teen back in Dayton. He was a known drug dealer by the name of Tyrell. Now, at this point of my life, I knew better. I was moving out of pure foolery. I was just hurt and confused, and my image of church and people had been tainted. I didn't care.

As soon as I began talking on the phone with Tyrell, I knew what this was about. I knew what he wanted. Plus, he was ten years older than me, which normally wouldn't be *toooo* bad, but in this situation, it was horrible. Most older men in the streets that I know of try to undermine or control you. But I went on with it, because I didn't care. I was truly going through a stage of rebellion. I was so disappointed in God and his people for that matter. I stopped going to church as much as I had been, just because I was fed up.

I got involved with Tyrell, and it was comfortable to me. His type was what I liked. For some reason, I always wanted a "project"—someone I could help Jesus fix, or deliver, if you will. I knew Tyrell wasn't right for me in the Christian sense, but in my mind, I just knew once again that he'd change for me, and we would have this not-so-perfect, perfect love story. That was my fairy tale.

Well, that fairy tale soon turned into a nightmare. The

more time we spent together over the course of five months, the more things got worse and worse by the month. One time we went on a date to the bowling alley, and the guy who ran the place was a black male. This man knew my mother, and I ended up speaking to him. When we had walked in, Tyrell walked past him and left, while the man and I started chatting. The guy asked me was if Tyrell was my boyfriend or just a friend. I told him that he was just a friend, and he responded, "Great. Keep it that way." I should have listened and not gotten myself too involved, but you live and you learn.

As I walked over to the table, I could see that Tyrell's eyes were bloodshot red, and he was looking at me with such disgust, as if I had done something wrong. He said, "You are a cheater." I didn't know where that had come from, considering that we weren't even in a relationship. He said, "I saw you flirting; I can tell in your eyes." He was very jealous, possessive, and insecure. I'm sure he was all those things because he was still doing his thing (talking to other females) as well. We didn't even live in the same city, and his lifestyle was such that I would have been a fool to think that I was the only female in his life.

I ignored his statement and just tried to enjoy myself, but the situation continued to go in a downward spiral. There was no consistency in this situation. *None!* When I had first met him, we talked all the time! But three months into this situation (which is not to be confused with an actual relationship), he drifted off and away. There was no honesty, no loyalty, no commitment.

I was chasing a false hope. I was hurt, so I was not thinking or looking through a clear lens. Instead, I saw someone who would take care of me; he was that "thug" I always thought I needed to handle me. In my mind, he was someone who could control me and my temper. He was everything I *thought* I wanted . . . or was he?

I had a very rude awakening coming. Because Tyrell stayed in Ohio, we traveled back and forth to see one another. I remember one occasion when I went to visit him. He liked to go bowling; it was like that was our thing. We were at the bowling alley, and he brought along his friend, Shaun. Shaun was also known in the city; he was a pretty boy and had a lot of women. He also was a drug dealer. I didn't like Shaun because he constantly ran his mouth like a female would, I felt.

I remember this one day in particular like it was yesterday. Shaun met Tyrell and me at Tyrell's house, and the three of us drove to the bowling alley. We were all bowling and having a good time and a few drinks, just hanging out, but Tyrell was extremely jealous. Shaun kept telling Tyrell how pretty I was, and I was standing right there. I said, "thank you" to Shaun. Tyrell looked at me as if I shouldn't have said a thing, and for the rest of the night he had an attitude. I didn't care; I just continued bowling.

We bowled a few more games, and then it was time for us to leave. Tyrell was continually bringing the Hennessey bottle to his lips, no chaser, once we had gotten back into the car. We were giving Shaun a ride home, so we pulled up to his house to drop him off—he was too intoxicated to be driving himself. Once we arrived, I asked Shaun if I could come in and use his bathroom—we still had a way to go to get to Tyrell's house—and Shaun said "Su—" when Tyrell rudely interrupted and said, "You can't wait until we get home?" with the most hateful look in his eyes. I said "*No!*" I had had a few drinks; my bladder was full and needed to be released. More importantly I didn't feel I needed nor had to explain that to Tyrell!

Shaun said, "Yeah, you can come in." I went into Shaun's house, used the rest room, came back out, and we left. As I reached for my seat belt, Tyrell's phone lit up. I was already on edge because of the way he had been acting the whole night. Now it's 2 A.M. and his phone is blowing up, three texts in a row! So, I snatched the phone from the middle console and started to read the messages. They were from a female. I instantly got *pissed* because there he was, acting crazy with me the whole night—and every time we visited one another, for that matter. All these thoughts came back to me, and I was livid.

I started to try reading all his messages. As I was scrolling, I said to him, "So who is this?" I probably had no right to act crazy because, one, we didn't live in the same city, and, two, we didn't have a committed relationship. I was probably emotionally attached because I had given him my body.

I started to try reading all his messages. As I was scrolling, I said to him, "So who is this?" I probably had no right to act crazy because, one, we didn't live in the same city, and, two, we didn't have a committed relationship. I was probably emotionally attached because I had given him my body. I was hurting myself because I had this idea in my mind of how things would work out, even though I knew in my heart all along that this wasn't the guy I was supposed to be with. Tyrell then yelled out, "*Give me my damn phone!!*" I yelled back "*No!*" He grabbed me by my face, somehow busting my lip by hitting it up against my teeth.

I dropped the phone on my side of the truck; I was determined to see what else was on it. I had long box braids at the time, all the way down my back to my waist. Tyrell grabbed my hair, wrapped it around his hand three times, and snatched me from the passenger side and over to his side, and he yelled in my ear, "*Bitch, give me my damn phone!*"

"*No!!*" *I yelled* back.

Why didn't I just give him back his phone? I'm not sure! But I know that I couldn't believe what had just happened, with him putting his hands on me. That was only the beginning. He put his car in park, opened his door in the middle of the street, got out, and walked over to my side of the car. We were close to a ditch and there were lots of trees—that's all I saw because of how dark it was, with only a few houses pretty far off. When he got over to my side of the car, he opened my door and grabbed me by the neck with both of his hands pushing me down onto the armrest. He began to strangle me. Both of his thumbs were pressing as hard as he could on my neck, causing my air flow to get tighter and tighter. Because I had had a few drinks, every reflex I had was slow.

Once I realized that he was choking me, I could feel myself slowly drifting away. Once I felt that, he let go. I didn't hear or see anything while this was going on. When he finally let me go, I sat up coughing; it was as if I was coming up from drowning underwater. Everything in the natural was made audible for me to hear. I heard, "Stupid ass childish bitch, dumbass, I hate you, stupid bitch. You're too friendly. You never ask another man to use his bathroom!!"

I couldn't believe my ears. I wanted to retaliate, I wanted to fight him, but I couldn't move. He was in the middle of the street cursing, throwing things, yelling! "I'm going to go to jail out here playing with you, bitch, I hate you!! I hate you!!"

At this point, his voice got squeaky—he sounded like he was about to cry. He was a lunatic. I had no idea he was this crazy. I was in complete shock.

As Tyrell was yelling out all those bad words, it was like my whole life was flashing before my eyes—from the time I was a child up until now. Every time he said that "bitch" word, it was like my body took a blow to the stomach; it was like I was getting weaker and weaker. Those words he spat out hurt me more than him choking me, hitting me in the lip, or pulling my hair. It was like when he spoke, his words spit on me, even though he wasn't actually spitting saliva on me.

All I could do was sit there and watch him. After a while, I felt no emotion; I had drawn a blank. I couldn't believe he had done all of that just over my taking his phone. His true colors had in fact been revealed long before this. They were revealed all the times he got mad when I spoke to another man—or when we were around other people, he didn't want me to talk to anyone but him.

I was silent the whole way to his house, where my car was parked. When we got there, I got in my car and drove away. I went and stayed with my cousin for the night just to get rest before I headed back to Nashville the next day. That next morning, Tyrell blew my phone up. He called over and repeatedly, leaving voicemails, apologizing, saying he would never do it again. I bought none of it.

Once I woke up and got my things together, I headed back home to Nashville. About two hours into my drive home—about halfway—I received a text message (one of the Hart Ramsey Uplift messages I get sent to me every day), saying, "All things work together for good! Even unkind words spoken against you are like distasteful seasoning that helps your flavoring," I couldn't do anything but say, "Wow, God!!" Still showing no emotion, I drove home in complete silence. I had never done that before; not for a four-and-a-half-hour drive. Usually, I'm either on the phone, listening to music, or admiring the beauty of nature! I had complete tunnel vision; I didn't say a word. I was still in shock.

That event where he basically assaulted me took place early that Sunday morning around 2 a.m. It didn't hit me where I showed any emotion until Monday. I was at work, when suddenly, I saw myself being nearly choked to death, and being called all those nasty words. I literally blacked out and just saw these recurring events taking place in my mind. I tried so hard to fight the tears, but they were coming down so fast I had no choice but to run into the rest room and attempt to get myself together. Once I got home after work, I just fell on my face in the middle of my floor, and I cried and cried, and cried. It had finally hit me: 1) I could have lost my life, *but if it wasn't for God*!!!!! 2) I had experienced something very traumatic like never before; and 3) my little ego was bruised.

I've played hard for so long. I fought my ex-boyfriend (Eric) plenty of times. No one had ever disrespected me, at least not in this manner. Now, here I was at my weakest point asking God to help me. I didn't know what else to do. I prayed and asked to be healed. I was admitting my weaknesses. I came bare and unashamed. Once I had gotten it all out, I got up and pulled myself together.

I went on like this for the next week or so, bruised and broken. Each morning for the next two weeks, I woke up, and the first thing I said after opening my eyes was, "I hate him!" Sometimes I said it before I even woke up. When I realized that I was awake, I would go through a mini-depression. I didn't want to wake up. I had *no* option but to get over it because I knew better than to reach out to him.

After the first week, I realized it was a wrap and that I needed to heal. Even in my foolishness, God was still speaking to me. Every day I woke up feeling depleted, scorn, hurt, angry, hating Tyrell. I felt that way until I was healed. The second week I woke up and I kept hearing "*hot tea*" in my spirit every day. . . . "*hot tea*" I got to where I was combating that. When I would hear "*hot tea*," I would say, "My emotions are so jacked, I feel so hurt, I'm a woman scorned."

One thing I've learned is that when you are facing a situation, be it adversity of any sort, you must have the right frame of mind. I know that's easier said than done, but if I would have had the right knowledge of what to say when I was facing adversity, the healing of my mind probably wouldn't have taken as long.

I finally settled myself and just listened. "OK, God, what does this 'hot tea' mean? Why do I keep hearing the phrase?!"

He said, "That last situation, you drank too fast!"

I sat on that for another week.

I went back and said, "OK, Lord?! I drank it too fast; I'm over it. I need understanding on what you're saying, so what does that mean!"

He said, "You drank that tea entirely too fast! You jumped into the situation with this person, didn't really know him— at least not in depth, for that matter—and now these are the consequences. You've burned your tongue! *But*, in this . . . I am changing your taste buds!!!"

According to ReferenceDay.com, "Taste buds are constantly forming and dying, *Woman's Day* explains. These cells typically live ten days to two weeks; (Hints: the reason it took me two weeks to heal!!) therefore, once they are burned, they die. There is *no way* of bringing these cells back, but *new* taste buds *quickly* form, taking the place of the burned buds."

Listen reader, can I tell you that I was *healed immediately*!! God prompted me to get on my knees. I prayed that he would remove from my spirit everyone (every soul tie) I had ever been with physically and emotionally. I asked for him to not allow me to talk to anyone else relationship-wise unless *he* sent them! I didn't want to make any more wrong decisions. I didn't have time to continue to slip down the same slippery trap. I was over it, fed up.

It was truly a matter of the heart and mind, I had to make it up in my mind that I was truly done and wanted to be delivered from the same old cycle of toxic, meaningless, and purposeless relationships.

It did not take me long to heal, and I am truly thankful. I believe it was because I was obedient. I prayed and I was fed up with doing things *my way*. I was content with the journey I was on; I was going through the healing process. I was OK with that. I walked around now feeling weightless, knowing that God was taking care of me and helping me heal. Since then, I have never been the same.

God spoke to me throughout the course of my healing process (a week later) through some messages sent from the Hart Ramsey Uplift text messages that I kept. I hope they bless you as much as they blessed me:

- "Often what we want, and what we are ready for, are miles apart; so God needs time to close the gap! Give him time to grow you!" I started to try reading all his messages.

- "It's easy to let the wrong people in, but hard to get them out. Wrong people don't just leave your life, they must be evicted! (Might I add, this message came during the time when Tyrell had reached back out to me one final time, because they never just leave. They will always reach out and try to apologize a thousand times before they get the hint. That why it's important to stay strong and don't give in. *Evict them*!!!!!!)"

- "Never enter someone's life or allow someone to enter your life without defining the relationship. Know who you are giving access to."

- "God loves you, and his grace is greater than anything you know and can handle any experience you've ever been through."

- "Losing streaks aren't trials. They're messages from God and come to test your faith. Encourage, obedience, and order your steps!"

Part III: Promise

9
A Manifested Prayer

1 Peter 5:10
"And the God of all grace, who called you unto his eternal glory in Christ, after you have suffered a little while, shall himself perfect, establish, and strengthen you."

TO BE CONTINUED…………………..

Epilogue

A Letter to the Reader

Dear Reader,

God bless you, I pray that while reading my testimony you've been encouraged, uplifted, and motivated. We all won't have the exact same story. Some of you may have never been through any of the things that I revealed in the previous pages. That is OK, because that is why we are all different. We go through different things to be able to reach different people!! That is where the beauty of "not fitting in" or being "different" comes in!!

Whatever it is you've been through, whether it is—abuse, neglect from a parent, divorce, domestic violence, abortion, people in church hurting you, or toxic relationships, just to name a few—you do have a story, and you won't be the same after one encounter with God. You are special and you ought not to take that lightly.

If you are reading this book, God wants you to receive what he has for you no matter what race, age, gender, or background you come from. It is never too late to turn from your old way of doing things and start moving as you should! Albert Einstein said doing the same thing over and over and expecting a different result is insanity. Don't go insane trying to make a system work that isn't meant for you! You might only need to be there to get the lesson and move on. Just push through. No matter where or what you come from, you don't have to live a defeated life.

Sincerely,

Da'Shay . . . A Kept Woman!

A Prayer

Father God, in the name of Jesus, I just thank you now for everyone who is reading this book.

Lord, I thank you for all the tests, trials, and tribulations that they've endured. I thank you for the pain and weaknesses, God, for that makes us stronger.

Lord, I thank you for all the setbacks, letdowns, hurt moments that they've all endured. I thank you that the pain is just weakness leaving the body!!

I thank you, God, because you're changing them in their pain.

God, you are magnificent, and we praise you for what you've done and who you are, before we ask you for anything. You are worthy, you are king of kings, you are a mind regulator, you are a heart mender, you are a friend, you are a mother, a father, a brother, and a sister. Thank you for being all we need, even when we don't know that we need it! Thank you for your grace and mercy.

Now, Father, I ask that you bless every person. Bless them, Lord. Send your angels of comfort to heal and break bonds and yokes, God, that have had them tied up for years.

Help their minds, Lord. We know that we can truly do anything we put our minds to! Literally!!

Help them get out of their own way of thinking. Give them the mind of you. Help them to not care what anyone else says, does, or feels.

Only you, Lord! Help them focus on what you want. You're all that matters. Be a shield as you've been for me, God. Watch over them as you have watched over me. Send your angels (people) and allow your divine intervention to work, so they can see that you are real!! Just as your word says, "Oh taste and see that the Lord is good, for his mercy endures forever!"

Allow them to taste your goodness as you've done for me, Lord. You sure are good!! I've tasted and seen, thank you, Lord, for being such a good God! You're such a great God! You're a deliverer!!! And a healer.

I am praying and believing, Lord, that you will send mentors to young girls, boys, mothers, and even fathers so that hearts are full and heavy burdened that need you.

Lord, they are thirsty for you! Send your power to rain down on them. Keep your hands on their life, Lord, don't leave them, they need you, Father!!

Thank you, God, that you're raising up queens who know their worth and kings who know theirs, and both who know their place.

Thank you, God, that the young women will keep themselves for that special one, and they will not cast their pearls among the swine anymore.

Thank you, God, that you are making them whole, and you are changing the minds of the young women and men now, even as they are reading this.

Thank you that you are emptying from them all the mess and clutter that gets in the way of your residing in them. Thank you, Lord, that they will never be the same.

God, you are amazing, and I praise you on their behalf, that everything I just asked and more, are already done.

Even before they pick up this book, you've already worked it out! Thank you for reminding them that you have a purpose for their life, and they don't have to settle for less than what you desire for them to have.

Thank you in advance for your healing power, and we believe it's already done.

In Jesus's name, we pray, we are FREE!!

Amen

About the Author

D A'SHAY ALISA PERRY, WHO IS FROM DAYTON, OHIO, AND NOW lives in Hendersonville, Tennessee, aspires to be a psychologist.

Because of the many adverse situations she experienced during her childhood and adolescence, she has become a woman of resilience. This is why she is able to inspire and motivate other people who are confronted with challenges similar to what she faced.